150

Great
AUSTRALIAN
Beers

For Tara. For your support and eternal patience.

ABOUT THE AUTHOR

James Smith was born in the famous brewing town of Burton upon Trent so this book was, perhaps, inevitable. It was three decades and a move to Australia later before he became fully immersed in beer, however. A journalist by trade, he began exploring and writing about the country's burgeoning micro-brewing culture soon after arriving in Melbourne in 2008. Since christened 'Crafty' in reference to his website, The Crafty Pint, he writes about beer for a number of publications and is a founder and festival director of the annual Good Beer Week festival in Victoria.

ACKNOWLEDGEMENTS

Countless column inches, books and blogs have directly or indirectly contributed in some way to this book. But it is more the time spent in the company of the people that have changed the Australian beer landscape over the past 30 years that has made it possible. Scores of brewers, writers, bar owners, beer judges, reps and educators have been incredibly generous with their time (and beer) and patient in the face of unrelenting (and, hopefully, steadily less idiotic) questions from this Brit who appeared one day and said he was going to write about craft beer in Australia. To acknowledge one and all, or even a good portion, by name would be more than anyone would want to read.

Instead, a few, starting at the start with Tom and Kate Delmont for picking up two strangers outside the Greyhound Hotel in St Kilda and taking them for a perception-altering visit to Mountain Goat in Richmond just weeks after landing in Melbourne and, in turn, to the Goat crew for subsequently inviting me on many of your adventures. Thanks to the brewers who have opened up their homes as well as their breweries to me and my family, and to Brad Rogers, Jamie Cook and co at Stone & Wood, who, six years in, still maintain a 100 per cent record of serving fresh Pacific Ale from their brewery tanks to every visiting member of the Smith family from overseas, immediate and otherwise.

A nod to everyone who has contributed to or assisted with The Crafty Pint in some way, particularly Nick Oscilowski and Pete 'Prof Pilsner' Mitcham, and to the entire Good Beer Week team for agreeing to take leave of their senses to create something from nothing. Josh Uljans, Tiffany Waldron, Miro Bellini and, above all, Shawn Sherlock have been invaluable sounding boards for this book, with the last also offering me the chance to brew a beer commercially. David Cryer has been a level-headed sounding board for pretty much everything else, Matt Kirkegaard a much-valued devil's advocate and mental sparring partner, and Shane Edwards has been, well, Shano.

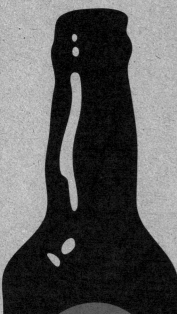

PALE
ALES

IPAs

BRITISH
AND IRISH
ALES

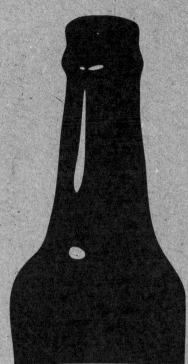

RED AND AMBER ALES

BROWNS, DARKS & PORTERS

STOUTS AND IMPERIAL STOUTS

BELGIAN STYLES

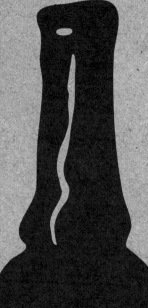

WHEAT BEERS

SPECIALTY BEERS

OTHER
BREWERIES

INDEX

HOW TO USE THIS BOOK

Beer style

ABV strength

Brewer's suggested serving temperature

Brewer's suggested serving vessel

Beer in Australia: An Introduction

If you are a 20-year-old in Australia today who enjoys drinking the occasional tasty beer, you may well wonder what all the fuss is about. You may question why many people older than you become so passionate when the subject of beer is raised, their passion manifested by an unstoppable desire to convert people to craft beer – or by the manner in which they decry the actions and products of the country's two dominant, foreign-owned brewing companies with the sort of language usually reserved for deviants and war criminals.

You may question why people who have long outgrown their band T-shirts have a collection of clothing that is adorned with cartoon hop flowers and the names of breweries from all over the world. After all, you don't see wine aficionados sauntering the country's wine regions with the names and logos of their favourite biodynamic winery emblazoned across their chests.

You may ask these questions, and more, with good reason.

'What's the big deal?' you might ask. 'I can get Little Creatures IPA, Stone & Wood Pacific Ale and Mountain Goat at my local Liquorland. What on earth are you getting so worked up about?'

The simple answer is this: if you are a 20-year-old in Australia today who enjoys drinking the occasional tasty beer, you're bloody lucky.

At the risk of sounding like an octogenarian bemoaning their great-grandchild's decision not to vote, a lot of people sacrificed a heck of a lot to get even that small selection of beers into the country's largest retail chains. Okay, so no one had to die

(though some of Australia's craft beer pioneers didn't live long enough to see the industry approach critical mass) but the struggle to brew, then sell and, ultimately, popularise anything that wasn't 5 per cent pale lager beer has been arduous. The growth of the microbrewery industry in the past five years has been so rapid that newcomers, and indeed most in the media, might feel it is an overnight success. Like most overnight successes, however, it has been a long time in the making.

Go back just five years and you will find plenty even within the beer industry who questioned whether craft beer's upward trajectory was sustainable or whether it would prove a flash in the pan. Go back 20 years and the number of breweries in Australia was barely in double figures; today there are more than 200 breweries and brewing companies. Go back just over 30 years and, with the exception of Coopers and a handful of old-school stouts, beer culture in Australia was a monoculture: one beer brewed by a handful of powerful state-based breweries, consumed by male drinkers loyal to their local brands and those of their dads and their dads before them.

THE ORIGINAL 'CRAFT' BEERS

Yet it was not always this way. Back in the early days of the colonies, breweries were local and brewed a range of beers, such as English-inspired ales, porters and stouts. The stories of the country's first two acknowledged brewers, James Squire and, to a lesser extent, John Boston, have been retold via contemporary brands that bear their names but, as settlers spread across Australia, breweries sprung up with them. The standard of their output may have been variable – brewers may have particularly struggled in the heat of summer due to a lack of refrigeration – but these small breweries, without distribution networks, would serve a handful of local outlets and offer a variety of beers.

With these local beers available alongside ales imported from England, Australian drinkers through much of the nineteenth century had a reasonable choice of tipples. Towards the end of the nineteenth century there were around 300 breweries in Australia – at a time when the population was still fewer than four million.

Change was coming, however, with its genesis towards the end of that century. Some of the larger, city-based breweries had begun establishing tied houses: pubs that they owned and that would only serve their beer, a tactic that gave them an advantage over many smaller, suburban and regional breweries. These challenges were exacerbated by the economic depression of the 1890s, during which many breweries closed.

It wasn't purely economics that threatened the existence of many smaller breweries, either. Drinking habits were to change, too. Gambrinus, a brewer from Germany, set up shop in Melbourne in 1885 and started brewing the country's first lager, bringing with them the means of refrigeration that allowed them to serve their beers chilled. Two years later, the American Foster brothers followed suit, with Castlemaine opening in Brisbane before the decade was out. As these breweries grew, the popularity of ice-cold, pale lagers – ideally suited to the hot Australian climate – took off.

The passing of the *Commonwealth Beer Excise Act* in 1901, which imposed heavy penalties on brewers who failed to meet its regulations, posed another threat to smaller breweries and led to further closures. While they shut their doors, the larger breweries with better technology, distribution networks and, ultimately, greater economies of scale, expanded rapidly. The shrinking of the industry was dramatic. According to *The Breweries of Australia*, by 1910 there were 157 breweries operating in Australia; a decade later that number had dwindled to just 77.

BEER'S PEAK AND NADIR

Fast forward to the 1970s again, and rationalisation had reached its peak – or nadir, depending on which side of the fence you sit. Beer consumption was at its highest level in Australian history and beer had the greatest share of the total alcohol market in the country. But punters were drinking that one beer, and they were drinking it in pubs that were generally rough, poorly maintained and purely the preserve of men. (Sure, there would be a room somewhere for the ladies to knit and sip Stone's Ginger Wine, but the front bar was for blokes. Should a woman venture in and assert her right to remain, she faced arrest.)

The industry was dominated by a handful of large breweries that serviced their home states, the likes of Castlemaine Perkins, CUB, Tooheys, Swan and the South Australian Brewing Company, each of whom focused predominantly on brewing one style of beer consistently and efficiently.

Imported beer was practically non-existent, certainly outside a handful of traditional Irish pubs and the Lowenbrau Keller in The Rocks. Towards the end of the 1960s, even the previously ale-only Coopers Brewery in South Australia had released its first lager in more than a century of unbroken brewing.

'Beer was nothing more than a fast-moving consumer good, and any discussion about quality or flavour was secondary,' says Phil Sexton, one of the pioneers of Australia's craft-brewing renaissance, of the period.

Australia was not alone in experiencing this change. Globally, large, efficient brewers of pilsner-style beers dominated. And if anyone had wanted to set up a smaller brewery they would have struggled. In Australia, when the major breweries upgraded their equipment, the redundant gear was destroyed to ensure there was no secondary market. And no manufacturer of brewing equipment anywhere in the world built anything suitable for a microbrewery setup.

However, the first stirrings of a beer renaissance had begun elsewhere. In the UK, the Campaign for Real Ale (CAMRA) was on the rise, trying to save and then re-popularise Britain's real ale tradition. And, in the US, Fritz Maytag had taken over Anchor Steam Brewery, which had started brewing beers such as the hoppy Liberty Ale; famous names such as Sierra Nevada, which was founded in 1980, were soon to follow.

A NEW BEGINNING

Inspired by time spent in the UK and Europe, and visits to some of the US's fledgling craft breweries, Sexton, along with hang-gliding mates from university, Garry Gosatti and John Tollis, felt compelled to rejuvenate Australia's bleak beer landscape. They first turned Fremantle's dilapidated Freemasons Hotel into the Sail & Anchor, complete with its own microbrewery, then built the original Matilda Bay Brewery. The full story of how this happened and their remarkable success is told elsewhere in this chapter, but in the years that followed they were joined by other pioneers.

In 1986, American brewmaster Chuck Hahn opened Hahn Brewery in the Sydney suburb of Camperdown and began brewing an authentic pilsner called Hahn Premium. The same year, Blair Hayden returned from the UK and started pouring English-inspired ales at the Lord Nelson in The Rocks. Geoff Scharer, who died in 2012, began brewing Scharer's Lager at Scharer's Little Brewery at the George IV Inn in Picton, New South Wales. Other small enterprises sprung up elsewhere but, of those to commence brewing in the 1980s, only these and Grand Ridge in Victoria, which started brewing in 1989, are brands that continue to this day.

Problems such as under-capitalisation and poor or inconsistent product meant that many ventures in this first wave of Australian craft breweries were short-lived. Matilda Bay was bought by Fosters at the start of the 1990s, and Hahn was snapped up by Lion Nathan (now Lion) in 1993, with the Camperdown site renamed the Malt Shovel Brewery and becoming the home for the James Squire range of beers under Chuck Hahn's guidance. While CAMRA enjoyed success in the UK and the American craft beer revolution took hold, Australia appeared to have suffered a false start.

That said, Coopers was on the rise. The brewery began producing draught beer for the first time in the 1980s, a decade that also saw the company take ownership of several hotels through which they were able to sell their beers, a move that mirrored the Matilda Bay approach to retail. A handful of imports from Europe and North America were becoming available to those who wanted to hunt them down and, with Matilda Bay and James Squire offering alternatives (albeit alternatives that were still owned by major breweries), there was a semblance of choice.

What Is Craft Beer?

As you make your way through the list of 150 beers in this book, a couple of things become quickly apparent. Firstly, none of the country's dominant brands appear: there's no VB, no Carlton Draught, no XXXX, no Tooheys. Secondly, the vast majority of beers featured are brewed by the country's small breweries, those that make up approximately 1 per cent of the entire Australian beer market and are widely referred to as 'craft beer'.

However, this is not a book solely dedicated to craft beer (otherwise it would be called *150 Great Australian Craft Beers*). When compiling the list, beers were selected predominantly because they are good examples of their style and are enjoyable to drink. An attempt was made to include as many breweries as possible, selecting the best or most interesting beer from their range, and there are one or two that feature because of what they stand for, such as Red Duck's Ra Egyptian Bread Beer, included as possibly the most extreme outlier of the experimental beers some of Australia's contemporary brewers are attempting.

But what is 'craft beer'?

It's a debate that has been held many times, and one into which I have always been reluctant to wade. Some have created definitions, and by pretty much all of them Hahn Premium Australian Pilsener is not craft – but, following its reinvention, it's a tasty drop. Indeed, if you go by the definition of craft beer as laid out by the US Brewers Association, then nothing from Little Creatures can be regarded as craft following its takeover by Lion, as it is no longer 'independent' of a major brewery. By the same argument, nothing from Matilda Bay is craft and neither is anything bearing the James Squire label. Yet going purely on flavour, many beers bearing those brands are of a higher quality than many produced by small breweries, and are also produced to a far greater level of consistency.

The debate over what is craft and the definition of what should be regarded as 'Australian craft beer' is one of the reasons why we currently have two, rather than one, craft brewing associations in this country. So, clearly, it matters. Or does it?

Ownership, output, ingredients used, authenticity and other factors are considered by those attempting to define what 'craft' really is. However, the best definition I've ever heard was put forward in a conversation with the country's leading beer writer-turned-brewer, Willie Simpson of Tasmania's Seven Sheds. It goes to the crux of the issue while also leaving room for manoeuvring as, in many ways, it is a subjective matter: what is authentic to one person will be different for someone else.

'It's the vibe,' he said, recalling that classic statement from *The Castle*. 'It's the vibe,' he repeated.

And, really, it is.

A tiny number of breweries that still operate to this day did open in the 1990s: Last Drop in the Perth Hills and Bootleg Brewery in Margaret River, for example. But it was not until the end of that decade that microbrewing in Australia began to grow in earnest. In the last years before the millennium, some of the most respected names in craft beer in Australia today released their first beer: Mountain Goat in Melbourne, Nail Brewing in Perth, and Holgate Brewhouse in Woodend, Victoria.

Perhaps the biggest single moment that kickstarted the second wave of craft brewing in Australia, however, was an echo of the very first. Phil Sexton, who had returned to his first love, wine, had also spent time in the US helping create BridgePort Brewing Company out of Columbia River Brewery, and was enticed back to Australia by former colleagues from Matilda Bay. Nic Tromboli and Howard Cearn saw an opportunity to start another brewery in WA, driven in part by displeasure with the direction in which Fosters had taken their earlier creation.

They opened Little Creatures on the Fremantle waterfront, a spectacular venture in a building that formerly housed a crocodile farm. It took the brewpub concept to another level in Australia and also brought with it a beer that was to revolutionise the country's drinking habits. Originally called Little Creatures Live, then renamed Little Creatures Pale Ale, this US-inspired ale featured the wonderfully aromatic, citrusy hops of the Pacific Northwest and was based on the hoppy pale ales and IPAs that were leading the charge for American craft brewers, tweaked by Sexton and fellow winemaker Janice McDonald for the Australian palate.

While growth of craft beer remained steady rather than spectacular and its market share was negligible, the early years of the new millennium saw a steady growth in the number of breweries, many opening up in popular wine and tourism regions – among them some now recognised as among the best in the country, including Feral Brewing in Swan Valley and Bridge Road Brewers in Beechworth.

Often they were opened by people who had experienced beer epiphanies while travelling through the US, the UK or Europe, and decided to change careers. But there were also those who were starting to view small-scale brewing as a viable career option. The number and diversity of quality imports available in Australia continued to rise too, opening palates and minds to the possibilities inherent in beer.

Despite this, there were plenty who doubted beer could follow the same trajectory enjoyed by Australian wine from the 1980s onwards. Commonly tagged 'boutique beer' (a term that could not be less appropriate for describing the ethos or, indeed, the personalities, of many involved in the Australian microbrewery scene), it was frequently written off as a fad that would die a similar death to the first wave.

The doubters had plenty of ammunition. It was a challenge for these breweries to find venues that would stock their beer, while a lack of brewing knowledge and ordinary equipment contributed to beer of a quality that was variable at best for many of the start-up breweries. Even a few years ago, you could find breweries that were seemingly founded on a belief that their point of difference and location in a popular tourism region would be reason enough for people to visit and drink their beers – quality be damned. Indeed, one suspects some owners figured (with good reason) that Australian beer drinkers wouldn't know what many of the styles of beers they were claiming to brew should taste like and thus wouldn't know whether they were good or bad. As long as it tasted 'different', it might be enough.

However, despite the naysayers, grow it did. What was increasingly being tagged 'craft beer' was taking off in many other countries. Information on techniques, new beer styles, new ingredients and more was being shared freely on the internet, giving brewers unprecedented access to a wealth of previously unavailable or hard-to-source information. In Australia, there was also a vibrant home-brewing culture developing. And a handful of visionary bar owners realised what was happening and resisted the temptation to take lucrative contracts or deals from the major breweries and instead operated as free houses, filling their taps with beers from these small local breweries. Suddenly, brewers had a means to get their beer to the public even if they didn't have a cellar door or brewery bar of their own.

As the availability of craft beer grew, so did the breadth of styles available either by import or from local breweries. Standards improved and, as beer drinkers became more knowledgeable about what various beers should taste like and started expecting more, there was less room in the market for substandard beers from local breweries. A handful of breweries closed, but in most cases they just began making better beer or brought in new brewers who could. By 2010, an industry that had been growing steadily for a decade began expanding faster and faster. Since then, growth in every aspect has been little short of phenomenal. It is not uncommon to find breweries reporting 100 per cent year-on-year growth, even several years into their existence. At times, it feels like there must be a small flotilla of ships making its way to Australia all year round, bringing nothing other than stainless steel fermenters and brewhouses from Europe, North America and China to satisfy Australians' voracious appetite for better beer.

Perhaps the best example of this phenomenal growth is Stone & Wood. The brewery was only opened in Byron Bay in 2008 by three mates who had previously worked in various roles at CUB, latterly at Matilda Bay where head brewer Brad Rogers was responsible for creating a series of eye-catching beers, including Australia's first commercially released saison, Barking Duck, and Alpha Pale Ale, a US-inspired ale that was named Champion Australian Beer at the 2013 Australian International Beer Awards.

The trio combined a smart business approach with a locally focused, grassroots touch, and their industry-changing Pacific Ale became the most striking success of the past decade. The beer, born of a careful analysis of 45 vastly different beers by the three mates – looking for every element they liked and disliked, then working out how to combine their findings in the perfect beer – has taken over Little Creatures Pale's mantle as the most recent to change the Australian beer landscape. Originally called Draught Ale and intended for their local market around Byron Bay, word soon spread and they were unable to resist demand. Now it is even sold in London.

Predominantly due to the Pacific Ale phenomenon, they ran out of space in their original home, despite clever use of every available inch, and have built a new, much larger, second brewery in the Northern Rivers region after spending months telling retailers, including the country's biggest, they simply could not meet demand, even when brewing 24 hours a day.

But they are far from alone in working frantically to meet demand. As sales for many of Australia's biggest brands continue to falter and overall beer consumption steadily declines, the clamour for the best local beers is so high that brewers struggle to meet their own state's demands, and have to bat away requests from eager bar owners and drinkers elsewhere. It is not uncommon to ask a brewer how things are going since their new, larger setup was installed and discover they have already exceeded capacity again and are bringing forward plans for the next stage of expansion. Some brewers have been forced to find alternative means of brewing their beer, outsourcing production of some of their main lines, at least in packaged form, to external operators that specialise in brewing for other businesses.

BEER NOW

Today, there is a truly multifaceted industry outside the world of commercial lagers that reaches into most corners of Australia. There are the brands owned by the two major brewers, Lion/Kirin (Little Creatures, James Squire, Kosciuszko) and CUB/SABMiller (Matilda Bay); independent breweries with extensive national reach such as Stone & Wood, Mountain Goat and, from the Gold Coast, Burleigh Brewing; a growing number of breweries with varying levels of regional and national distribution; and the many who are content to serve their local market with little desire to grow, who would rather drinkers come to see them at the cellar door than send beer in the other direction. And then there is the family-owned Coopers, in a category all of its own.

There has also been a third wave of brewers. By this, I mean brewers who entered the industry with little regard for perceived norms, in their own way doing what Phil Sexton, Chuck Hahn, Geoff Scharer and their ilk did in the 1980s, but in a rather more twisted manner. Inspired by the 'no rules' ethos of many American brewers, they ignored what was seen as the sensible approach – essentially, create a core range featuring something approachable like

a golden ale and back it up with something fruity (a wheat beer), something a little hoppy (pale ale) and something darker (porter or stout) – and instead did it their own way.

Sure, by this stage there were many breweries across Australia producing innovative and often unusual beers as limited releases, but not as their entire output from day one. Kickstarting this third wave was Moon Dog. Based in a small industrial unit in Abbotsford, equidistant between CUB's headquarters and a brothel, their first official releases were a barrel-aged wild black ale featuring cherries called Perverse Sexual Amalgam and a cognac barrel-aged imperial IPA called Skunkworks. Today, the two brothers and their mate that started the brewery have finally deviated a little towards the norm (with three core beers available year round where once they released nothing but single batches that may or may not be repeated), but they continue to push the boundaries with most of their beers, their names and their labels.

Their success has inspired others to leap straight into the deep end too, launching with beers that are close to their hearts rather than those they believe would have reasonable mass market appeal.

It is not just the beers available that are changing. As more young brewers look to turn their dreams into commercial reality, they are seeking ever more creative ways to break into the industry. There used to be pretty much three choices: find half a million dollars or more and build your own brewery; come up with a brand and pay someone else to brew for you; or cobble something together from repurposed milk and cosmetic vats or tanks intended for winemaking.

More recently, however, some have branded themselves as 'gypsy' and 'nomad' brewers – those without their own equipment who travel from brewery to brewery, creating their beers on other people's gear.

And now there is another way. A small number of 'communal breweries' are starting to flourish around the country. Some created by design, others more by accident, they are typically owned by one brewery that invites other brewing companies to buy their own fermenters to be installed alongside their host's. The brewing companies brew on the host brewery's equipment but have their own space in which to ferment and condition beer without tying up their host's capacity. Young Henrys in Newtown has offered space to The Grifter Brewing Company, allowing three talented young brewers a foothold in the market they otherwise would not have been able to afford. Cavalier in Melbourne's west has a horde of brewers beating a path to their warehouse, among them BrewCult, Kaiju!, Boneyard and Dainton Family Brewing. In Adelaide, Big Shed Brewing was set up with this approach in mind; the owners 'rent' their brewery and fermenters to other brewing companies.

Other notable trends include collaboration brews, the rise of specialist beer bars and an explosion of beer festivals, both in the form of beer weeks and one- or two-day events that bring together brewers with their own stalls alongside food and wine producers, usually with bands playing on a main stage.

It is only a few years since Australia's first collaboration brew, but now they have become a common way of marking a special occasion or allowing visiting brewers from overseas to leave a parting gift. Or just because. Local brewers have created beers with guests from the US, Europe and New Zealand, with many travelling the other way to return the favour.

At times, these collaborations have gone to extraordinary lengths, never more so than in a series of brews created by Bridge Road Brewers' Ben Kraus and Kjetil Jikiun of Norway's famed Nøgne Ø. Among the many collaborations they have created are the Aurora Borealis and Aurora Australis I and II. Both involved the brewers in Australia and Norway creating strong Belgian ales as a base beer, placing them inside one of four different types of barrels and sending them unrefrigerated via the ocean to their collaborating brewery, where they would be blended, bottled and released. Some barrels have exploded along the way, but currently Aurora Australis I is the highest-rated Australian beer on global online beer geek hangout Ratebeer.

Collaborations have not been limited to brewers either. Producers of other alcoholic beverages, non-alcoholic beverages and food products, and bands, writers, surfers and many more, have been invited to share their creative concepts with brewers. Even I was lucky enough to conceive a beer for commercial release, a smoked imperial Belgian mussel and oyster stout called Auld Bulgin' Boysterous Bicep brewed with Murray's in New South Wales, which may have received a second release by the time this book is published. In many ways, this trend highlights the open and inclusive nature of beer. It does not depend, like wine, on factors such as terroir or seasonal variation. Barring shortages, which do occur with popular hop varieties, brewers can conceive pretty much anything, then source the ingredients required. Provided they are skilled enough, they can turn even the wildest of ideas into a great beer.

It is not just Australian brewers making their mark either. Over the past decade, Hop Products Australia, the country's largest grower of commercial hops, has changed tack significantly to focus on creating a greater number of aroma and flavour hops. Some, particularly Galaxy and Ella, are in great demand the world over.

The concept of the specialty beer bar, such as the Wheatsheaf Hotel (aka The Wheaty) in Adelaide, the Clancy's Fish Pubs in WA and The Local Taphouses in Melbourne and Sydney, has also experienced a phenomenal rise. Perhaps more importantly for the future growth of the craft beer industry, an increasing number of 'normal' pubs and bars now stock nothing but small-brewery beers, or at least the more interesting brands from the bigger players. Good beer is also finding a home in more and more restaurants.

As for the festivals, where once there was a small number of one- or two-day beer festivals in the annual calendar, now – particularly in summer – they are found all over the country. Not all are successful yet, but the likes of the Tasmanian International Beerfest, Ballarat Beer Festival and the Great Australian Beer Festival in Geelong are showing how they can be.

A more recent development is the beer week. Just as WA was the first state to have craft beer, it was the first with a beer week, although the one operated by the state's brewing association was, until recently, a small, niche affair. The arrival of Good Beer Week in Melbourne in 2011 took things to another level. Initially run in conjunction with the long-running Australian International Beer Awards, but now also incorporating Australia's Craft Brewers Conference and the huge Great Australian Beer SpecTAPular within its nine days, it has become an event with global reach, regularly enticing brewers from five continents to Australia for an array of events celebrating beer and beer culture in every way imaginable. (Full disclosure: I am a co-founder and festival director of Good Beer Week.) It has spawned city- and state-based beer weeks in Sydney, Brisbane, Canberra and Hobart, as well as the five-day Good Beer Wheaty in Adelaide.

Taken together, along with a number of major trophies for Australian beers in international competitions, it is safe to say that there has never been a more exciting period for the beer industry here. The market share for beer from the country's 200 small producers remains staggeringly small – around 1 per cent – but this just means potential for further growth is huge. Brewers face growing challenges, not just internally in terms of growing pains, but externally. As word has spread about Australians' insatiable appetite for better beer, the amount of incredibly high-quality imports arriving here has grown exponentially. Similarly, the big boys are realising this is not a fad that will one day curl up and die.

Lion took total control of Little Creatures in 2012 and also now owns Emerson's in New Zealand, one of that country's trailblazing micros. Thus far, however, all other significant independent brands have resisted outside approaches. Notably, when the Lion takeover of Little World Beverages (the company that owned Little Creatures and White Rabbit) took place, it gave them a share in Stone & Wood. Following a series of meetings and some soul-searching, Rogers and his business partners Jamie Cook and Ross Jurisich opted to buy back that share and thus become fully independent. Whether all others will choose the same route in the future, only time will tell.

The major retail chains have joined in the fun, too. Woolworths took a significant share in WA's Gage Roads and, while Gage Roads continues to brew its own range of beers and contract brews beers for others, it also produces beers under the Sail & Anchor label, effectively Woolworths' home brand. Coles has followed suit, creating its own range of beers under the Steamrail mantle.

Opinion is divided as to whether this is good for the craft beer industry and, indeed, whether such beers can be called 'craft' (the debate on what exactly craft beer is being one that has been run many times). What these moves by the major retailers do suggest is an attitude of: 'If you can't beat 'em, join 'em.' And that in itself should be reason for even the most ardent critic to celebrate.

After all, only a few years ago, many still questioned whether craft beer would take hold in Australia, even the second time around. Now craft beer is, without a doubt, here to stay. Mainstream media is still often misinformed, but the tone is becoming slightly less patronising with time and you can even, on occasion, walk into small restaurants in country towns and find a section in their drinks list headed 'Craft Beer'.

After lagging behind Melbourne for many years, the sleeping giant that was Sydney has finally come alive, aided by a rising number of small breweries and a thriving small bar scene, while those that questioned until very recently whether Brisbane would ever have even a single bar pouring craft beer now have their own weeklong beer festival, Brewsvegas, to celebrate. All six states have their own small brewing industry, each with their own unique character, while one of the country's best brewing minds, Richard Watkins, calls Canberra home. The man who started it all in Fremantle more than three decades ago says that, were he 10 years younger, he would start another brewery in Australia today.

It may have taken far longer than Sexton or many who followed in his footsteps ever imagined, but Australia once again has a beer culture worthy of the name. As with many other nations around the world, we have rediscovered what beer was always about and are taking it in unimagined new directions.

In years to come, this period will be looked back upon as one of the most significant in beer's millennia-long history. Hopefully, the twentieth century's industrialisation and commoditisation of this wonderful beverage will in time be looked upon as nothing more than an unfortunate blip in its evolving 10,000-year story, and beer will continue to enjoy the valued role in society and civilisation that it has always held. All of which sounds like cause for a celebration. Cheers!

The First Craft Beer

Towards the end of 2012, Lion announced that it was closing WA's Swan Brewery, which had been operating in Perth for more than 150 years. Maybe things would have turned out differently, both for Swan and beer in Australia generally, if those in charge at the brewery had listened to one of their young brewers three decades ago.

Young winemaker-turned-brewer Phil Sexton had spent time in England in the late 1970s and early 1980s, studying for a master's degree in biochemistry. He studied with equal fascination the small breweries and brewing techniques of the Midlands where he was based and became involved with the fledgling Campaign for Real Ale (CAMRA). He also visited breweries in Belgium and Germany and, well aware of the changes afoot in the US, was alive to the possibilities the brave new beer world could offer.

Upon returning to Western Australia, he informed his bosses at Swan what was happening, and suggested they look into brewing some alternative beers. The response, he says, was blunt: 'Shut up and go back to work.'

Convinced that the changes taking place in the beer world elsewhere would at some point reach Australia, and knowing he was interested in making beer with flavour and authenticity, he

and two university pals, Garry Gosatti and John Tollis, drew up a business plan for a new kind of brewery. After leaving Swan, he tried pitching the idea to Castlemaine in Queensland. They too threw him out.

Undeterred, the hunt for backers continued in WA. The hunt eventually led to Peter Briggs, a colourful property developer–turned–gold mining entrepreneur, yachtsman and racing car enthusiast, who was later to spend time in prison for tax evasion. They were warned not to deal with him but also learned that he had recently bought a brewery with the intention of taking the fight to Swan Brewery, before eventually selling the site to Swan for a price he couldn't refuse.

Despite the warnings, the young entrepreneurs met with Briggs and found him keen. According to Sexton, all he wanted to know was: 'Can this guy cook?' And, once Briggs was convinced, he agreed to fund the venture, which involved purchasing a brewery from Robert Morton DG in the UK, the first business to start manufacturing small-scale brewery equipment at the time, on which they proposed brewing a high quality pilsner.

According to Sexton, there was no contract, merely a simple request from Briggs: 'Don't dud me.'

Their mission was far from over, however. They were able to place an order for a brewery but needed to ensure there was a market for their beer when it arrived. This, again, proved impossible. No venue would risk angering Swan, so they faced the prospect of potentially having the best beer in Australia – and no one to drink it.

The solution was to buy their own pub. Their search brought them to the Freemasons Hotel in Fremantle. At the time, Fremantle was a far cry from the happening waterfront town it is now. It was rough, and so was the Freemasons. It was available, however, so Sexton, Gosatti and Tollis returned to Briggs and suggested he buy it and then lease it to them. He did, and they set about giving it an overhaul. Out went the 'skimpies' – women working behind the bar in a state of near undress – the place was cleaned up, and beers otherwise unavailable in the state, such as Coopers Sparkling Ale, were lined up for the taps.

As they waited for what was to become the Matilda Bay Brewery to be built, they constructed another brewery on the site of what they had renamed the Sail & Anchor. And there Sexton brewed Australia's first modern craft beer in late 1984.

It was the Anchor Special Bitter, as classic an English bitter as one could wish to find: brewed with Maris Otter malt and Fuggles and Goldings hops, all imported from England. It was 4.2 per cent ABV, dry hopped, slightly cloudy, used isinglass finings for clarity and was primed in casks. They installed stillage racks for the casks and soon the pub was 'pumping'.

Because it was female friendly, the women flocked. And where there were women, the men wanted to be, too. When Matilda Bay came online, they began brewing their authentic pilsner, using softened water, 100 per cent imported Saaz hops, low-nitrogen barley and a triple decoction mash. Before long, they were going through 150 kegs in a week and had opened a second venue, The Brewery Alehouse.

Among other beers to pour at their venues was Carlton Draught. To contemporary drinkers, this may seem a rather strange move, but back then breweries would not step onto another state brewery's patch. Through a friendly retailer, they secured a supply and people started crossing town to drink it. It was, says Sexton, 'like going to the girl's toilets', something weird and, perhaps, a little naughty.

Despite the fact pretty much the entire Australian beer industry was intent on stopping them, their success continued unabated. Within three years, they had more than 30 retail outlets across Australia and had set up the Specialist Beer Company to bring in the likes of Stella Artois, Moosehead from Canada, Young's from the UK, and Bitburger from Germany. Matilda Bay Brewery was constantly being upgraded and expanded. According to Sexton, what they did 'broke the nexus'.

Other factors played a role. Australian society had been changing throughout the 1970s under the Whitlam administration – the role of women was evolving and the country was becoming more multicultural – so the climate was ready for something new. There were events outside the Matilda Bay team's control that helped too, not least Alan Bond bringing the America's Cup to Fremantle in 1987 and the support they gained from the local Orange People.

'They were already outlaws and had made Fremantle their home,' says Sexton. 'They were there because they objected to something and suddenly here was a group of young guys trying to do something completely different with everybody against them and they massively supported us.

'Basically the crowds followed them. They were a countercultural movement and we needed that mass to get moving. Otherwise we would have been a spectacular failure.'

Instead, they were a spectacular success. And despite the fact that members of the original Matilda Bay were to repeat this success in 2000 with Little Creatures, Sexton remains keen to play down their role and instead play up their luck: a case of right time, right place.

'The stars aligned in many ways,' he says. 'It was when rock 'n' roll was real!

'We weren't clever. We were just surviving.'

How Beer Is Made

Stripped back to its very basics, beer is a remarkably simple thing. It is made of four ingredients: malt, water, hops and yeast. A wide variety of those four ingredients is available to brewers anywhere in the world, pretty much whenever they want them.

The process of combining those four ingredients to make beer is also, when stripped back to its very basics, remarkably simple. Malt is milled, then mashed in hot water to extract fermentable sugars. This sweet water is then boiled and hops are added before it is cooled and transferred to a fermenter where yeast is added. Over the course of a few days, it turns into what we know as beer.

The easiest way to think of it is like cooking: brewers follow a recipe and add the right ingredients at the right time to achieve the desired outcome. In fact, you can brew a beer on your stovetop at home using exactly the same ingredients as a commercial brewer.

Yet there is good beer and bad beer, so it can't be that easy, right? Furthermore, as you will discover while making your way through the 150 beers in this book – which only represent a small percentage of the beers released in Australia in any one year – those four ingredients and that simple process can lead to vastly different outcomes.

There is a huge variety to choose from within each of beer's key ingredients, and they can be combined in any way a brewer sees fit. Even changing the make-up of the water can alter a beer. Likewise, any variation at any stage of the brewing process – be that the temperature of the water in which the malt is steeped in the mash tun; the length of time the sweet water (known as wort) is boiled in the kettle; how much, when and what type of hops are added; the temperature at which fermentation takes place; or even the vessel in which fermentation takes place – can change the character of the beer.

In reality, there are endless possibilities with these four ingredients, and this simple process, and the science, techniques and art of brewing, can become as complex as a student of beer wants it to be. But, for the purposes of this book, let's keep things as simple as possible. First up, the basics of the brewing process...

THE BREWING PROCESS

Almost all beer begins with malted barley (see the ingredients section opposite). A brewer will mill (essentially crush) their chosen blend of malts and add it to a mash tun where it will be mixed with hot water that is heated to a temperature dependent on what beer is being brewed. This process converts the starches in the malt into fermentable sugars that are dissolved into the water to form a sweet, sugary liquid known as wort. Usually, it takes about an hour to convert the starches into malt sugars.

At this point, the sweet wort is slowly separated from the grain in the mash tun, using the grain bed itself as a filter (in a process known as lautering). Water is slowly poured over the grain, in a process known as sparging, to ensure as much of the fermentable sugars have been extracted as possible. Once transferred to the brew kettle, the liquid is heated to boiling temperature.

It is here that hops are first added (except in very rare cases when brewers choose to add hops in the mash tun in a process known as mash hopping). Hops added early in the boil will give a beer bitterness, while those added towards the end of the boil, which typically lasts around 90 minutes, will lend beer flavours and aromas. (See the section on hops on page 22 for more.)

The boiling process can also aid clarity and the long-term stability of the finished beer by 'breaking' proteins that then drop out of suspension.

Once the boil is complete, the liquid is cooled rapidly, usually via a heat exchanger, and transferred to a fermentation vessel. It is at this point that the sugary, hoppy liquid will be transformed into beer. This happens when the final of the four key ingredients is added: yeast. These microscopic living organisms go to work, multiplying rapidly and devouring the fermentable sugars. As they do so, they create two useful byproducts: alcohol and carbon dioxide, as well as adding a range of flavours and aromas.

Several days later, the yeast's work is done and a brewer has beer. Some types of beer will be packaged at this point and sent straight into the market for consumption. Often, however, a brewer will allow a beer to condition longer in the tank, as this additional time allows yeast to settle out, leaving an end product with much greater clarity.

The vast majority of commercial beer is filtered, and in some cases pasteurised, before being force carbonated with carbon dioxide and transferred into kegs or bottles. In some cases, particularly among craft brewers, beer undergoes a secondary fermentation in bottle or keg, meaning live yeast remains in the beer so that it continues to develop and retains its spritzy carbonation.

THE INGREDIENTS

Malt Malt, or malted barley, is beer's backbone – the source of the sugars that will be fermented into alcohol, and most of its flavours, too. In today's rapidly evolving craft-beer world, many drinkers are first lured in by hops, with their dramatic aromas like a light bulb to a moth. But while you can create beer without hops (in fact, beer existed for millennia before humans were even aware of hops), you cannot create beer without malt, water and yeast.

The vast majority of beers are brewed using varieties of malted barley. Once harvested, it goes through a process of steeping in water and then partial, controlled germination to encourage the production of enzymes and starches. After four or five days, and before the germinating grains begin to grow plants, they are kilned (or dried) to create malt. What type of malt is created depends on how long they are kilned for, at what temperature, and how much moisture is in the air (or indeed in the grains themselves) when they are kilned by the maltster.

The most commonly used base malts in beers are the palest; in other words those kilned for the least amount of time at the lowest temperatures. As malts become progressively darker, the flavours, aromas and colour they lend to a beer change accordingly. While the lightest of malts used alone will give a brewer pale-yellow or light-golden beers and lightly sweet, sometimes honey-like, flavours and aromas, as you move along the scale, malts will lend beers colours that range from copper, amber and red to various shades of brown and, ultimately, black. Flavours and aromas move from those akin to biscuit to caramel, nuts, chocolate and treacle to coffee and even fairly harsh, acrid roast bitterness, with many shades in between.

Malted barley may be the most common grain used in beer, but it is not the only one. Many beers also use a percentage of wheat, both malted and unaltered. It is found in high proportions in wheat beers (see the Wheat Beers chapter) and also in small amounts in other beers where it can help a brewer achieve a particular body, assist with head retention or add a dryness or tartness. Rye malt is becoming increasingly popular among craft brewers too. It gives beers a fuller, almost oily or slick, body, as well as adding a distinct and intense spicy flavour. Another ingredient often found in a grain bill is oats, particularly in stouts, where they help create a smooth, silky and creamy body. Brewers, particularly large commercial brewers, will also use rice and corn on occasion, often as adjuncts designed to affect the body of a beer as well as, to an extent, its flavour.

Then there are smoked malts. These fall into two main categories. There is the malted barley smoked over open wood fires, with beechwood the most popular fuel. They have been popularised by German brewers, with the best known of these being Schlenkerla. As well as lending a sweet smokiness to beers, the flavours and aromas are commonly described as meaty, in particular bacon-like.

Some brewers also use peated distilling malt on occasion. As the name suggests, this is a type of malted barley typically used by whisky distilleries. It is produced in peat-fueled kilns and comes in a range of intensities. Many brewers would run a mile rather than have such grains in their brewery due to their potency and persistence but, used in small amounts, they can add additional layers of character and complexity to a beer. In a couple of extreme cases, brewers have created beers using 100 per cent peated distilling malt, including Tasmania's Seven Sheds with its Smokin' Bagpipes.

In addition to these varieties, malt companies around the world are constantly developing new 'specialty malts'. Sometimes these are designed to give a particular colour to a beer without adding much in the way of flavour, including one known as Midnight Wheat that has become increasingly popular as a means of creating deeply dark beers without the associated roast or bitter flavours.

These days, it is worth adding that nothing is off-limits for brewers. Across the globe you will find limited-release beers using grains that are native to a particular area or ancient grains that may have been used to make beer hundreds or thousands of years ago. And then there are varieties such as sorghum and millet that are essential to the handful of brewers specialising in creating gluten-free beers for coeliacs. In 2013, Ballarat-based O'Brien Beer won the first-ever gold medal awarded to a gluten-free beer in Australia.

Hops Hops are a relative newcomer to the world of beer. Historians and archaeologists have found evidence of brewing and beer consumption in the Middle East and former Mesopotamia stretching back several thousand years. Yet the earliest recorded use of hops in beer is ninth-century France. Prior to that, a wide variety of herbs and other less savoury ingredients – soot, anyone? – were used instead.

The easiest way to understand what they contribute to beer is to return to the cooking analogy. Hops are like spices. They are added in the latter part of the brewing (or cooking) process and used predominantly for three reasons: to add bitterness, aroma and flavour to a beer. They have other useful properties, not least acting as a preservative, but it is those three roles in which they specialise.

The hop plant, Humulus lupulus – literally 'wolf in the woods' – is cultivated on hop farms. Hop bines grow up strings attached to trellises and can reach up to around 3 metres in height. The parts that are of interest to brewers are the flowers of the female plants: bulbous, yellow-green cones that are harvested in early autumn. They grow between 35 and 55 degrees of latitude in both the northern and southern hemispheres, with the most famous hop-growing regions found across France, Germany and the Czech Republic, in Southern England, in the Pacific Northwest of the US, the north of New Zealand's South Island around Nelson, and in the Victorian High Country and Bushy Park in Tasmania.

At harvest time, they are dried within hours of being cut from the trellises and are processed into one of a number of different formats. These include whole hop flowers, hop pellets, hop extract and hop oils.

As stated earlier, their primary use to a brewer is to deliver bitterness, flavour and aroma. The point at which hops are added in the brewing process dictates what characteristics a brewer will obtain. Adding them early in the boil, once the sweet wort has been transferred from the mash tun, delivers predominantly bitterness via a process called isomerisation, which occurs from boiling hops, typically for a period between one and two hours. Much of the flavour and aroma is lost to the atmosphere from hops added early in the boil. Those added later, either towards the end of the boil, after the boil or during or post fermentation, contribute little in the way of bitterness but instead deliver flavour and aroma. Part of the brewer's skill is to capture just the right amount and balance of these different characteristics from the hops.

Many contemporary craft brewers favour adding large amounts of hops late in the process, after the boil has been completed. This can be in a whirlpool or hop back (vessels through which the sweet, hoppy wort passes on its way to a fermenter), or in the fermenter itself in a process known as 'dry-hopping'.

The bitterness that hops lend to beers is measured on a scale called International Bitterness Units or IBUs. The human palate is said to be unable to detect an increase in bitterness beyond 100 to 120 IBUs, but this hasn't stopped some extreme brewers creating beers with theoretical bitterness levels in the hundreds, even one that claimed to have 1000 IBUs. Ultimately, however, any good beer will have a balanced bitterness wherein even if the number of IBUs is high, the perceived bitterness on the palate is balanced by malt sweetness.

As for the aromas and flavours a drinker can expect from hops, it depends on the variety. Certain common characteristics can be expected from hops native to certain regions of the world. The world's oldest and biggest hop-growing region, centred around southern Germany and surrounding countries, produces hops known for their subtlety and elegance, often possessing soft spice and lemon citrus aromas and flavours. Four varieties from the region are known as noble hops, originally developed in the wild, which are low in bitterness and high in aroma. They are Hallertau, Saaz, Tettnanger and Spalt, and many contemporary varieties have been developed from their parentage.

English hops are traditionally known for their floral and earthy nature and can give beers a gentle, broad and lingering bitterness. Those developed in the Pacific Northwest of the US are typically much more powerful, known for their pungent citrus, grapefruit and pine aromas and flavours, as well as an assertive bitterness.

A number of recently developed varieties of Kiwi hops are known for their tropical aromas, such as lychee and kiwifruit. One particularly distinctive variety is named Nelson Sauvin because of its similarity to sauvignon blanc grapes. Australian hop growers have been relative latecomers to the move towards aroma hops, but in recent years Hop Products Australia has developed a number of new breeds that are proving hugely popular throughout the beer world, with the passionfruit-like Galaxy leading the charge.

To understand the different aromas and flavours particular hop varieties can lend to a beer, some brewers have created single-hop series, including Bridge Road Brewers from Beechworth and 4 Pines Brewery from Manly. For these, they create a beer that is identical in every way – grain bill, alcohol content and yeast – but change the hops. For the most part, however, brewers will use a blend of different varieties at different stages in the brewing process to achieve balance and complexity of the flavours and aromas they desire.

Yeast Without yeast there would be no beer. Yet for most of beer's history, brewers of beer in its various historical forms had no idea that such a thing existed. They just knew that, given the right ingredients and certain conditions, the process that we now understand as yeast cells consuming fermentable sugars and creating alcohol and carbon dioxide would turn those ingredients into something that, when imbibed, would make them feel warm and fuzzy. Natural yeasts in the environment were doing the work for them.

Yeast is so central to beer, and indeed the creation of great, clean beer, that you will often hear brewers refer to themselves as 'yeast farmers'. By this, they are highlighting how their most important role, aside, perhaps, from recipe development, is creating the perfect conditions for their chosen yeast to go to work and turn sugary, hoppy water into wonderful, aromatic, flavoursome and balanced beer.

This means using healthy yeast (yeasts can be pitched and re-pitched into beer, but they will mutate if used over long periods of time). And it means creating an environment free of potential contamination, and at an appropriate temperature where these unicellular organisms can multiply and feast.

As you will discover later in the book, different yeast strains will add a range of nuances to beer. Lager yeasts are typically described as 'clean' and, like many American ale yeasts, are 'neutral'; in other words they add little in the way of flavour or aroma to a beer. English ale yeasts are known for the fruity characteristics they impart, while Belgian ale yeasts – those found in saisons, witbiers, dubbels, tripels and quadrupels, for example – as well as the yeast strains used in German wheat beers such as Hefeweizen, are responsible for some of the most dominant characteristics in those beers: typically a range of fruits and spices.

Different yeasts prefer different temperatures at which to operate, something that is touched upon in the introduction to the chapter on lagers. Typically, lager yeasts go to work between 8°C and 12°C, ale yeasts between 18°C and 22°C. But, while an individual yeast strain may have a preferred temperature range in which it would like to operate, brewers can play around with this to achieve different results in the end beer. In the hands of a skilled brewer, 'stressing' yeast by maintaining a temperature that is cooler or warmer than it would prefer can lead to some interesting and welcome flavours in a finished beer.

Water While brewers do not have the vast array of options with water that they do with malt, hops or yeast, how they treat their water can affect the outcome. Different compositions of water in terms of its mineral content and acidity or alkalinity are best suited to different types of beers. This is best highlighted in a couple of classic beer styles.

The water in Pilsen, in the Czech Republic, is incredibly soft – not far from being as pure as filtered water. It is perfect for brewing pale beers, as during mashing brewers are able to reach the desired acidity for turning starches into fermentable sugars using just pale malts. The result is beers with soft malt flavours and aromas that allow the aromatics of noble hops, such as Saaz, to shine unhindered. The pilsner style born there has gone on to dominate the world of beer.

Conversely, the water in Burton-upon-Trent, in the heart of England, is hard. Its natural composition allowed the town's brewers to create paler, more assertively bitter, ales than their peers in London in the nineteenth century, leading to a period of dominance for Burton's brewers. A chemist later discovered how to reproduce the water's mineral content, a process named Burtonisation, so that brewers anywhere could create such pale ales.

There are other examples of beers developing in part due to an adaptation to the natural water of particular area, such as Guinness in Dublin, where the water is not suited to producing paler beers. Today, with the importance of water's composition fully understood, brewers anywhere can use a range of key salts, such as calcium sulphate, calcium carbonate, sodium chloride and calcium chloride, to manipulate the water profile to suit the beer they intend to brew.

Serving and Enjoying Beer

To get the best out of your beer, it should be served in optimum conditions. This can mean using an appropriate glass and drinking it at the right temperature. Better still, it should involve drinking it in the right setting and, ideally, with good company.

If this sounds a little over the top for beer, for which the choice of serving vessel has traditionally been stubby or can, pot or pint, then consider this: would you serve ice cream warm, on a plate, with a fork? Have you considered offering houseguests a pot of tea in which the teabags have been suspended in cold water straight from the tap? Would you serve shiraz cold in a tumbler?

The point is that beer, at least beer brewed to be savoured, should be treated no differently than any other food or beverage. Steadily, Australians are waking up to that fact and are beginning to appreciate the diversity, versatility, quality and complexity inherent in good beer and according it similar respect to that granted to everything from wine to cheese to coffee. Once that is understood, it makes perfect sense to want to serve and enjoy every beer in the best way possible.

When you read through the list of 150 beers in this book, you will see that the brewers of each beer have recommended the ideal temperature at which they should be enjoyed, as well as the most appropriate glassware. And, while I'm not suggesting you carry a thermometer and a padded rucksack containing a range of glassware with you at all times, where possible it is worth paying attention to their suggestions as they will make a difference to the quality of your experience.

Perhaps the most important rule when it comes to choosing the appropriate glass for a beer is this: use a glass.

I describe a number of different glass types below, but simply by using a glass rather than drinking straight from a bottle or can, you instantly enhance your appreciation. To fully enjoy a beer, we must engage our entire olfactory system, as what we actually taste via our taste buds – sweet, salt, bitter, sour and umami – is only a small percentage of the overall experience. Those tastes without the accompanying aromas tell only a tiny part of the story.

Think back to the last time you had a cold. Your nose was blocked and your head was stuffy: did food taste the same or did it appear bland? In effect, by drinking beer from a bottle or can you are creating for yourself that same handicap: locking in the aromas and only allowing yourself to experience a piece of what the brewer intended. Once the beer is poured into a glass, it opens up and releases those aromas in full: fruity, spicy, or earthy hops; sweet, nutty or roast malts; fruity, herbal, or peppery esters from the yeast. If a brewer is going to the trouble of creating a beer with aromas that could encompass orange blossom or coriander, pine cones or sherbet, lychees or leather, clotted-cream toffee or Vegemite, it's just rude to keep them under virtual lock and key.

The second most important rule when it comes to glassware is to ensure it is clean. This may sound like a case of stating the bleeding obvious, but with beer it is particularly important. Residue, even that left by washing-up liquid, can kill a beer's head, which isn't there just to look pretty but plays host to the aforementioned aromatics. A beer's head can also act as a form of 'liquid bottle top', protecting the beer in your glass from the unwanted effects of oxygen.

Beyond this, it depends how far you want to go. If you have room for just one beer glass in your cupboard, the best option is to go for some form of goblet with room in which to swirl the contents and release those all-important aromas. If you do wish to take things to another level, there are glasses designed for certain beer styles. Glassware manufacturers such as Spiegelau run eye-opening master classes that demonstrate the difference style-appropriate glassware can make to carbonation, aroma, mouthfeel and so on.

There are specialist, beer-specific designs out there if you wish to stock up at home and serve every beer as the brewer intended. Some of the best-known and iconic style-specific glasses include those used for German weissbiers: they're tall, curvaceous, almost voluptuous, affairs designed to maintain the beer's thick, fluffy head. Pilsner glasses are traditionally tall and thin, highlighting the colour and clarity of their contents.

In Belgium, where beer is held in higher regard than any other country, you find some of the most beautiful glassware. Many brewers produce their own large, stemmed, tulip-shaped goblets designed to make the most of the beer's wonderful aromatics and retain its foamy head. Trappist breweries have their own particular design of glassware that is akin to a chalice. Some look almost too good to drink from, as if they should be perched on your mantelpiece; that is, of course, until you sample the beer for which the glass is intended and realise nothing could be too good for it.

More recently, Spiegelau released a unique IPA glass, designed in conjunction with US breweries Dogfish Head and Sierra Nevada, which has a series of ripples or bumps in its lower half. This has been followed by the development of a specialist stout glass, created with two other US breweries, Rogue Ales and Left Hand Brewing.

Of course, while you may wish to dedicate an entire shelf to a range of glassware, any clean, stemmed wine glass will ensure your beer-drinking experience is far superior to merely knocking the cap off a bottle and glugging straight from the neck.

For the most part, when drinking in a pub you'll be handed a standard pot, schooner or pint glass. None are designed with any great focus on showcasing aromas and flavours at their best; the flip side is that, in most cases, if you're drinking at the pub the priority should be socialising rather than in-depth analysis of the contents of your glass. That said, many specialist beer bars have started using stemmed tulip glasses, while a handful even have some high-end glassware for use with their fanciest tipples.

As for temperature, it also plays a significant role in the enjoyment of beer. The colder a beer is, the less its aromas and flavours come into play. For pale lagers and pilsners, this is less of an issue as they are generally clean, dry beers – but serving many other styles too cold means locking away much that is good about them. Thus, particularly with richer, heavier, darker beers, it is best to remove them from the fridge and allow them to warm a while before consuming them.

Each beer listing in this book includes the brewer's preferred serving temperature, and that is the best guide for maximising your drinking pleasure. With the more complex beers you will also notice the flavours and aromas changing significantly as they warm in your glass.

STORING BEER

With the vast majority of beer styles, the mantra 'fresh is best' is apt. More often than not, a beer will never taste better than the first day it is tapped, ideally at a bar at the brewery where it has been brewed. This is particularly true with lighter and hop-forward beers, with hop aromatics the first thing to fade in a beer in the months after it is released. Beer is also affected negatively by heat and light, so the best place to store it if you're not consuming straight away is in your fridge.

That said, there are certain beer styles that are designed to age and that can develop greater complexity and interest over time. These include strong Belgian ales, barley wines and imperial stouts and porters. Ideally, to mature these beers they should be kept in a cool cellar but, given most Australian homes don't come with cellars, the coolest, darkest spot you can find in your home may have to do. Alternatively, an extra fridge set at warmer, cellar-like temperatures would suffice. I know my wife loves the fact I have two fridges for beer.

Beer and Food

*J*ust as beer has come a long way from the days when choice meant 'Do you want one or not?', so has the concept of beer and food pairing moved on from pairing a snag in one hand with a tinny in the other.

Today you can invite someone to a beer dinner without expecting a response along the lines of 'Is that like a liquid lunch?' And, mercifully (if painfully slowly), it's getting rarer to flick past a 20-page wine list in an acclaimed restaurant only to alight upon a beer list comprising eight nigh-on-identical European-style lagers and a light beer – the equivalent of such a restaurant being proud to offer an exhaustive range of cask wines, although only, of course, white varieties.

Now that Australian drinkers are faced with a wonderfully diverse range of beers from which to choose, both brewed locally and imported from across the globe, they have an incredible range of flavours, textures and aromas to match with food. Where once there was a tiny number of advocates banging the drum for beer to be treated with similar respect to wine on the dining table, now it is not uncommon to find the occasional beer creeping onto leading restaurants' degustation menus, or chefs and brewers joining forces to combine each of their specialist subjects into a culinary feast.

Of course, just as craft beer is not something new, merely a renaissance of how things used to be (albeit with the condensed knowledge of thousands of years and with added bells and whistles), the pairing of beer and food is no modern invention. In fact, while brewers and advocates for better beer will use high-profile dinners as a means of showcasing beer to new and wider audiences, when you examine some of the classic pairings you'll find origins that stretch back long before Fritz Maytag bought Anchor Steam in California and kickstarted the modern craft-beer revolution.

Beer has been enjoyed with food for as long as it has existed. The difference now is the level to which beer and food pairing, and indeed cooking with beer, is sometimes taken. But, whether it is a drinker at home deciding which beer to pull from the fridge to have with dinner, or a brewer, sommelier and chef conferring in a hatted restaurant ahead of a degustation, the guiding principles remain the same. Ultimately, just as a brewer seeks to achieve balance in a beer, the aim when pairing beer and food should be to achieve balance, too.

Rather than attempt to explain how to do this with words and theory, this book offers 150 ways to understand how the two can work together in practice. As with serving temperature and glassware, the brewers of most of the beers featured here have suggested their favourite food match. By attempting these pairings yourself, your palate will tell you what works.

That said, armed with a few basic principles, you can begin to understand just why those pairings work and attempt to create your own.

One key consideration is assessing the weight or intensity of a particular beer or a dish that you intend to pair with beer. Beers that are lighter on the palate will pair better with lighter dishes, such as seafood with a Hefeweizen or witbier, while something heavier, such as a smoked brisket, sits perfectly with the rich, heavier malt flavours of a porter. Switch them around, and the porter would overwhelm a light seafood dish; the gentle sweetness and spiciness of either wheat beer would be no match for the meat.

When considering weight or intensity and beer, there are a number of aspects to consider, including bitterness, level of alcohol, richness, sweetness, carbonation and so on. Similarly, when assessing food, it is not just the core ingredient but also how it has been cooked or prepared, the heat or spices that have been added, and the texture, too.

You will often hear people talk about the 'three Cs' when discussing beer-and-food pairing: complement, contrast and cleanse. Keeping these in mind is another simple way to plan successful marriages.

Complement means finding common characteristics between what is on your plate and in your glass. This could be as obvious as the rich, dark malt flavours of an imperial stout with bitter chocolate or a fruity Belgian beer with a sweet, fruity dessert. Or it could be more subtle, perhaps a hint of orange zest within a sauce that reflects the citrus hop flavours of a particular beer.

Beer can also be used to contrast certain elements of a dish to create a balanced whole. Pairing a dry Irish stout with raw oysters is a classic for a reason. Pairing a sweet, malty brown ale can take the edge off a hot chilli dish. Interestingly, there are many who advocate combining hoppy ales or IPAs with hot, spicy dishes; such beers intensify the heat, particularly as alcohol content and bitterness rise, something that may not be to everybody's liking, but which appeals to heat fiends.

When it comes to beer's cleansing properties, it can work in a number of ways. Highly carbonated beers can make heavier dishes seem lighter; similarly, well-hopped beers have the ability to cut through fatty, creamy or oily foods, refreshing the palate. Beers with high acidity are excellent for countering salty foods.

Another phrase you may hear in relation to beer and food matching is 'What grows together, goes together.' When you think of such tried-and-tested traditional pairings as a German weissbier with weisswurst, commonly enjoyed with a pretzel as a late-morning snack throughout Bavaria, there is an appeal that is both evocative of a time and place and delicious on the palate.

With beer offering up such a vast and complex array of flavours, aromas and textures, there are endless possibilities when it comes to beer and food pairing. And, while there are classic matches and guiding principles, there is little that beats experimentation.

As for the beer versus wine question that often raises its head: why not beer *and* wine? Within the broad spectrum of each, you can find characteristics that they share and others that are unique to one or the other. Certainly, the caramelised flavours that you can find in many beers is absent in wine and opens up many excellent pairings, while there are heavenly matches that wine can achieve with certain foods that beer cannot. In fact, once one heads down the path of seeking out perfect pairings to elevate both the beverage and cuisine to a higher plane, surely the only logical conclusion is to bring every single beverage into play. Not just beer, not just wine, and not just beer and wine.

There are books dedicated to the art of beer and food pairing, most notably *The Brewmaster's Table* by Garrett Oliver, for those wishing to take their understanding deeper. Another way to enhance your appreciation is to look out for the many beer dinners held regularly throughout Australia, particularly at the growing number of beer weeks taking place in most cities. Often the chef or host sommelier or brewer will be on hand to talk through their decision-making process.

Then there is self-exploration, and not just in the kitchen either. There is plenty to be said for picking up a selection of beers, some artisan cheeses and cured meats, and spending an evening seeing which work best together.

There is, of course, no need to devour books or work towards a PhD student's understanding of the science and theory behind why a saison works well with a particular washed-rind cheese. But, just as knowing a little bit about beer and its ingredients helps you enjoy beer a little more, so a little comprehension about how beer and food can work in harmony can enhance any meal.

If you do commit to exploring the world of beer and food, rest assured there will be revelations ahead. Perhaps it will be the first time you experience the right imperial stout with a chunk of creamy English stilton, or the moment a particular herb in a sauce sets off fireworks with the Belgian ale in your mouth. Whenever and whatever those matches and moments are, enjoy!

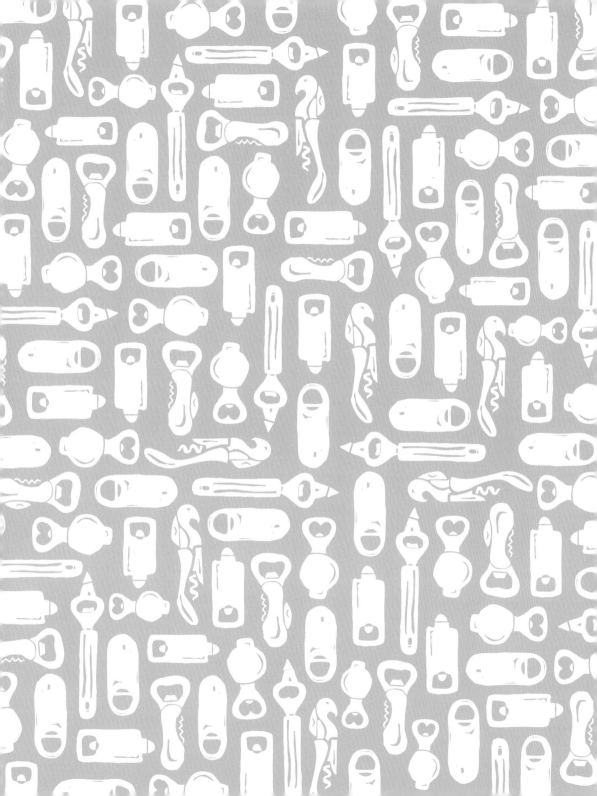

LAGERS

Lager

Of every ten beers consumed in Australia, nine of them are lagers. It's a pattern repeated the world over. Yet lagers make up less than 10 per cent of the beers featured within this book, as well as a small fraction of the total number of officially recognised beer styles.

The utter dominance – at least in terms of consumption – of lager beers in Australia, in particular pale lagers, is a legacy of the phenomenal growth of a handful of breweries that successfully captured the Australian market in the twentieth century. The local beer industry shrank from almost 300 breweries across Australia at the turn of the twentieth century to a bare handful by the 1980s; the choice of beer in your local pub became similarly limited, too: usually 'heavy' or 'light' from your state's main brewery.

This homogenisation of Australia's beer culture became possible for a number of reasons. Light lagers were well suited to the country's hot climate, thus those who had the ability to make them – and make them well and consistently – were at an advantage. Too many breweries were making poor and inconsistent beer, allowing those with the best technology and skills to thrive. Innovations in refrigeration helped these pilsner-style beers thrive too, with pubs and hotels able to serve them ice-cold.

The larger breweries also established their own extensive distribution networks and set up their own pub chains. These 'tied pubs' gave them the ability to lock their competitors out. And, as the rationalisation of Australian breweries reached its peak (or nadir), each state's dominant brewer would focus on its own market, leaving its interstate peers alone to monopolise their local market in the knowledge that they, in return, would do the same. Thus when Phil Sexton secured Carlton Draught through a third party to pour at the Sail & Anchor in Fremantle in the mid-1980s, it became the only place pouring the popular Victorian drop in WA – and caused much consternation at WA's major brewery, Swan.

It was against such a backdrop that what has become known as the craft beer industry today began: as a rebellion against the commoditisation and mundaneness of beer, and a desire to create something other than commonly derided 'fizzy yellow lager'.

Yet three decades on from the opening of the Sail & Anchor and the work of the late Geoff Scharer, who brewed pioneering lagers in New South Wales at the same time, this alone does not explain the relative scarcity of 'craft' lagers and pilsners from Australia's 200-plus breweries and brewing companies.

Brewing a lager properly takes time – the larger brewers might be able to use special techniques to turn around commercial lagers in as little as six days, but six *weeks* or more is regarded as an appropriate conditioning time for a pilsner-style beer. Indeed, the very term 'lager' comes from the German 'lagern', which means 'to store' and relates to the period of weeks or months these beers spend maturing at close to freezing point. For many smaller breweries already working at capacity, such time is a luxury they simply do not have; ales can progress from raw ingredients to packaged product in less than two weeks. Furthermore, creating a traditional German-style lager or pilsner – typically clean, refined beers – leaves a brewer with nowhere to hide.

But what is lager, other than the beer poured from almost every tap at most pubs, hotels and sporting clubs in Australia? It is one half of the wider beer family, the other half being ale. And the one thing that distinguishes all lagers from all ales is its yeast.

Ale yeasts (*Saccharomyces cerivisiae*) generally ferment wort (see the section on the brewing process for further explanation) at relatively warm temperatures (15°C to 24°C), while lager yeasts go to work at lower temperatures (6°C to 13°C) and generally go about the business of turning wort into beer at a much slower rate. Lager yeasts also settle at the bottom of a beer, while ale yeasts are top-fermenting. For those of a historical bent, lager yeasts are known as both *Saccharomyces pastorianus*, named after Louis Pasteur, the chemist who discovered microbial fermentation (as well as vaccination and pasteurisation), and *Saccharomyces carlsbergensis*, in honour of Emil Christian Hansen, who first described the species when working for Danish brewery Carlsberg in the late nineteenth century.

So how does this help with your selection next time you're faced with a line-up of taps on a bar or several fridges full of bottles? The main difference when it comes to having a lager or an ale in your hand is that lager yeasts tend to deliver cleaner ferments. In other words, they give off less byproducts that are noticeable in the finished beer. Whereas a brewer would expect to gain some fruity characteristics from an English ale yeast or spices from a Belgian witbier yeast, for example, lager yeasts are more neutral, allowing the characteristics of the malt, hops and, to a lesser extent, water to take centre stage. Hence talk of 'clean' or 'crisp' lagers and pilsners.

This does not mean that all lagers, however, are pale, clean and/or crisp. The beers that have risen to dominance worldwide over the past century and a half, based upon the wonderful helles lagers from Bavaria and pilsners from the Czech Republic developed in the mid–nineteenth century, may suit such descriptors. Yet lager yeast can be used with any combination of grain and hops, creating lagers that are dark, rich and heavy, too. Indeed, before the first pale lagers were created in Munich in the nineteenth century, lagers would have, for the most part, been dark.

Today, darker variants include copper-coloured Vienna lagers and schwarzbiers (black beers), while bocks (strong lagers) and their bigger variants doppelbocks and eisbocks are usually darker as well as boozier.

The range of beers that fall under the broader 'lager' style can be seen in this chapter, which features pale pilsners, dark lagers, a dark coffee lager and even a luscious, nigh-on-black Baltic porter, originally a type of imperial stout brewed in Eastern Europe using a cold-fermenting lager yeast.

TOP OF THE HOPS

EDGE BREWING COOL HOPS
KNAPPSTEIN RESERVE LAGER
RED HILL BREWERY PILSNER

Kung Foo Rice Lager
2 BROTHERS BREWERY

 Rice lager **4.5%** **2°C**  **Pilsner**

TASTING NOTES This pours such a pale straw colour that the aroma can come as a surprise: citrusy, tropical fruits abound. Those characters dominate the flavour too, with the light, soft, sweet malts very much in a subservient role in this high-quality, light-bodied quaffer.

THE STORY There are plenty in the craft-beer world who get rather sniffy when it comes to the use of adjuncts such as rice in beer, given its prevalence in beers created by the Evil Brewers of Macro-lagers™. Look deeper and there are historical reasons for its use as well as the more sniffed-at reasons, such as its ability to lend beers a lighter body and colour and lessen the malt flavour – essentially, one might argue, making it less 'beery'.

At the same time, there are beers that make clever use of unusual rice types (like Hitachino Nest's Red Rice Ale) and brewers creating ales with rice in the US. And, as with everything when it comes to beer, it's the intention that counts. For Moorabbin's 2 Brothers, they may have stripped things down on the malt front, but they build it back up when it comes to the addition of hops. Certainly, no one who would run a mile to avoid drinking a Bud Light is likely to have grounds to grumble with the Bruce Lee–adorned Kung Foo Rice Lager; it's thanks to its delicate and clean baseline that the appealing tropical aromas can take centre stage.

Brewer's food match
Tempura prawns, char kway teow

Availability
Year round

Where to find it
2 Brothers Brewery, McCoppins (Fitzroy), Grain and Grape (Moorabbin), Valley Cellars (Moonee Ponds)

Brewery and cellar door location
4 Joyner Street, Moorabbin, Victoria

Brewery website
www.2brothers.com.au

Voodoo Baltic Porter
2 BROTHERS BREWERY

 **Baltic porter** 6.3% 6°C  **Tulip glass**

TASTING NOTES Wonderfully full and rounded, this beer pours dark brown with a blood-red tinge and has a mouthfeel that is nothing short of creamy. Hazelnut, vanilla, chocolate fudge and crème caramel abound, with an earthiness, even something slightly woody, on the back palate too.

THE STORY If there is one thing that Moorabbin's 2 Brothers Brewery does as well as collecting major trophies for its beers, it's creating beers for those of a malty – even sweet-toothed – disposition. The Voodoo Porter, which was the first of their beers to win a trophy at the Australian International Beer Awards, belongs in a high-quality cadre of full-bodied, luscious and high-ABV beers conceived by head brewer Andrew Ong.

You can file it alongside such big beasts as the Guv'nor (another trophy winner), the Terminator Doppelbock, the Magic Pudding dessert beer and funky Belgian James Brown. That said, it's the most refined of that bunch: a Baltic Porter – in other words, a big, rich, dark lager – that's like the proverbial iron fist in a velvet glove.

While this dark beer is called a porter or baltic porter, and is related to imperial stouts, it is cold-fermented with a lager yeast and, after chatting with its brewer, is thus listed in the Lagers section.

Brewer's food match
Key lime pie, pork belly

Availability
June–August

Where to find it
McCoppins (Fitzroy), Grain and Grape (Moorabbin), Valley Cellars (Moonee Ponds)

Brewery and cellar door location
4 Joyner Street, Moorabbin, Victoria

Brewery website
www.2brothers.com.au

Black Giraffe

BURLEIGH BREWING

 Black coffee lager   **5.0%**   **6-8°C**   **Snifter glass**

TASTING NOTES There can be few beers that squeeze so much action into a mere 5 per center. Seriously black and seriously balanced, freshly roasted Zarraffa's coffee joins fruity US hops and layers of chocolate malts in a dark lager as smooth as an expertly stretched flat white.

THE STORY There's something about hot and humid weather that can cause quite a turnaround in even the most fanatical craft beer aficionado. Corner such a person in Queensland on a steamy afternoon and they'll confide that XXXX Gold is a pretty decent drop. Try getting the same beer past their lips on a cool July day in Victoria and you'd have a battle on your hands.

Thus, when the Gold Coast's Burleigh Brewing added the Black Giraffe to their limited release schedule a few years ago, it was quite an eye-opener. Peruse the rest of their range and you'd find lagers, a low-carb beer, hoppy ales: beers designed for sessionability and warm weather. Yet here was a deeply dark affair created in conjunction with a local coffee roaster. But despite its roasty overtones and distinct coffee characteristics, this lager possesses the sort of immaculate balance that ensures it goes down easy, even in its home brewery's climes. No wonder it became one of the many Burleigh beers to pick up medals overseas and was named among the best in the world by *All About Beer* magazine.

Brewer's food match
Any winter meal; tarts and fruit pies such as apple pie or berry crumble

Availability
Seasonal

Where to find it
Focussed distribution in South East Queensland, but available Australia-wide

in selected liquor chains, independent bottle shops and a variety of bars and restaurants

Brewery and cellar door location
17A Ern Harley Drive, Burleigh Heads, Queensland

Brewery website
www.burleighbrewing.com.au

Pilsener

COWARAMUP BREWING COMPANY

 **German-style pilsener** **5.0%**  **4.5-7°C** **Pilsener glass**

TASTING NOTES This former trophy-winner is one of the punchiest pilseners you'll find in Australia. It presents beautifully, with a towering cloud of white head atop its bright golden body. Soft hop and sweet malt aromas lead into a silky body, where you'll find distinctive, hay-like hop flavours amid the malt sweetness before a clean and no-nonsense bitterness wraps up proceedings.

THE STORY The annual Australian International Beer Awards tend to throw up the odd surprise. Few moments in recent history, however, have been as surprising, or indeed as heartwarming, as when the pilsener from Cowaramup was announced the winner of Best Lager in 2011.

It was surprising for most people in the room, as few would have heard of the tiny Margaret River brewery run by expat Brit Jeremy Good. But it was surprising for Jeremy too, as it was a beer style he had only chosen to brew because he felt he needed a lager on his roster to win over the WA locals that weren't warming to his beloved English-style ales. It has earned the beer its own place in Aussie craft-beer folklore, not least because you still pretty much have to travel to the brewery to have any chance of finding it. That's no bad thing, as chances are Jeremy will be pouring the beers at the bar, only too happy to reminisce (possibly with a tear in his eye).

Brewer's food match
Grilled barramundi

Availability
Year round at selected pubs

Where to find it
Margaret River Hotel, Clancy's City Beach and Dunsborough, Goodfella's

Cafe Restaurant, El Rio Mexican Restaurant, The Goose, Knights Inn

Brewery and cellar door location
229 North Treeton Road, Cowaramup, Western Australia

Brewery website
www.cowaramupbrewing.com.au

Cool Hops

EDGE BREWING PROJECT

 **Australian lager**   **4.6%**   **6°C**   **Tapered pilsner glass**

TASTING NOTES A golden lager with a foamy white head, Cool Hops is an all-Aussie affair that offers up a healthy dose of alluring tropical and grassy hop aromas atop a soft and full malty base. Balanced and rounded out with a nice bitterness, it's a great example of a New World lager.

THE STORY In recent years, as the beer scene in Australia has transformed and the popularity of craft beer has exploded, more and more international brewers of note have beaten a path here. In 2012 you could barely move without bumping into another Scandinavian on a brewery tour, with each visitor taking time out to create a collaborative beer or three with anointed locals.

One of these visitors, Christian Skovdal Andersen of Beer Here, has taken things a few steps further and formed a collaborative venture by the name of Edge Brewing Project with his Australian importer, Adam Betts of Northdown. Their first Aussie release was this New World lager, which wasted little time after release in becoming one of the highest-rated lagers in the southern hemisphere. Christian didn't just lend his brewing nous to the project, either. He kindly donated his unique artistry to the labels too, with Cool Hops coming complete with the rather comical image of a hop flower wearing shades while surfing on a sea of beer.

Brewer's food match
Kingfish ceviche

Availability
Year round

Where to find it
Independent bottle shops and bars; on tap at The Beaufort, Some Velvet Morning and Clever Little Tailor

Brewery location
124 Railway Place, West Melbourne, Victoria

Brewery website
www.edgebrewing.com.au

Hahn Premium Australian Pilsener

HAHN BREWING COMPANY

 Australian-style lager based on German pilsener 5.0%  2-4°C  Tall pilsner glass

TASTING NOTES With its creator having headed back into the brewery and reworked this beer into something close to its award-winning early days, the result is a clear, pale-yellow beer with subtle floral, spicy and lemon hops mixing with soft grains on the nose, a touch of white wine–like fruitiness to taste and a gently building, refreshing bitterness to finish.

THE STORY These days, it is not uncommon to walk into a bottle shop and be faced with a selection of 300 or 400 beers, sometimes significantly more. Back in the late 80s, beer drinkers desiring something other than wetness and a mild buzz found their choices considerably more restricted. Then American-born brewmaster Chuck Hahn launched a brewery in Camperdown and released Hahn Premium, a pilsener based on Europe's finest, that made no compromise for Australian palates. It went on to win champion trophies, but in the years after Hahn was bought by Lion Nathan in 1993 it became something of a forgotten child, with greater attention paid to its Lion stablemates SuperDry and Boags Premium.

Late in 2012, Chuck decided it was time to revisit the beer that had made his name in Australia. On a visit to the brewery, he discovered that old, stale hops were being used and weren't being added as desired. A few tweaks here, an insistence upon fresh hops there, and the beer began heading back to its roots. The process of reinvention has continued and, while it remains harder to find than SuperDry, when you can locate it, it's well worth picking up.

Brewer's food match
Fresh seafood; weisswurst sausage and pretzels

Availability
Year round

Where to find it
Australia-wide

Brewery location
Lion, 68 York Street, Sydney, New South Wales

Brewery website
www.hahn.com.au

Reserve Lager
KNAPPSTEIN

 **Bavarian-style lager** **5.6%**  **2-4°C** **Fine pilsner or tall tulip glass**

TASTING NOTES At its best this golden, German-style lager gives off clouds of tropical fruit aromas – passionfruit, lychee, grapefruit – while making full use of the distinctive Nelson Sauvin hops from New Zealand. It's rich and creamy too, making it stand out from the mainstream lager crowd.

THE STORY Knappstein, in the Clare Valley, is first and foremost a producer of wine. Part of the Lion empire, in 2006 it added a wooden-clad microbrewery to the interior of its striking, redbrick home in the heart of Clare.

The brewery has only ever produced one beer, this Reserve Lager based on the clean, crisp lagers of southern Germany. That said, more recently a barrel-aged variant that gains soft vanilla characteristics from the oak has been released in tiny batches for special events and beer festivals. What's more, its popularity means that demand has outgrown its original home; although most batches are still brewed out of Clare, the supply is augmented by occasional brews at the Malt Shovel Brewery in Camperdown, home of the James Squire range of beers.

Brewer's food match
Fresh, spicy Thai food

Availability
Year round

Where to find it
Australia-wide in good bottle shops and restaurants

Brewery location
Clare Valley, South Australia

Cellar door
2 Pioneer Avenue, Clare Valley, South Australia

Brewery website
www.knappstein.com.au

Vale DRK

MCLAREN VALE BEER COMPANY

 **American dark lager** **4.5%** **4-5°C**  **Tulip glass**

TASTING NOTES This US-inspired dark lager has more going on than initially meets the eye. The use of the Falconer's Flight hop blend, designed with bigger, hoppier ales in mind, adds citrus and pine aromas to a subtly complex malt profile with touches of cocoa, coffee and caramel.

THE STORY McLaren Vale had a bumpy introduction to the Australian beer world. Not in terms of sales – with smart marketing and eye-catching branding seeing Vale ALE (the first and, for some time, only release) achieve significant success relatively quickly – but in terms of acceptance. Despite calling McLaren Vale home, initially all of its beers were brewed under licence interstate, a situation to which some took umbrage.

Today it brews draught beer at its own facility in Willunga, near McLaren Vale, while being open about where its bottles are produced, and has added several more approachable beers to its core range, with head brewer Jeff Wright also given free rein to concoct some more adventurous one-offs. Fresh on tap, their IPA has become perhaps their most loved beer, but this dark lager is more consistent across all formats.

Brewer's food match
Pork belly or chocolate brownies

Availability
Year round

Where to find it
All good retailers and selected hotels
Australia-wide

Brewery and cellar door location
6 Jay Drive, Willunga, South Australia

Brewery website
www.mvbeer.com

Dogbolter

MATILDA BAY BREWING COMPANY

 **Dark lager**   **5.2%**   **10°C**   **Tall glass tankard**

TASTING NOTES A dark lager that pours a glowing ruby-chestnut colour with a crema head, it has aromas of soft caramel and chocolate. Soft and full-bodied, it has a lovely, deep malt character that builds to a toasty, slightly roasty and rounded bitter finish.

THE STORY The current beer bearing the name 'Dogbolter' is a fine beer in its own right. A smooth and rich dark lager that lingers long on the palate, it currently resides within Matilda Bay's reserve range (in other words, it's harder to find than the core range). It would belong in any list of quality current Australian beers regardless, but has special significance because of its name.

The original Dogbolter brewed by Matilda Bay, back in its original incarnation in WA as the first craft brewery in Australia, was an 8 per cent English-style ale unique in the country at the time. Today, that long-retired beer has attained mythical status, with the current bearer of its name a rather different beast, just as the current Matilda Bay Brewery, part of SABMiller and based in Port Melbourne, Victoria, is a far cry from the one that began by supplying the Sail & Anchor in Fremantle and lit the touchpaper for the craft beer revolution.

Brewer's food match
Braised beef and chocolate tacos

Availability
Year round

Where to find it
Selected bottle shops

Brewery and cellar door location
89 Bertie Street, Port Melbourne, Victoria

Brewery website
www.matildabay.com.au

Stefano's Pilsner
MILDURA BREWERY

 Pilsner lager **4.7%** **4-6°C**  **Flute**

TASTING NOTES If this is Stefano de Pieri's tribute to his European ancestors, then he's done them proud. This bright yellow pilsner with the fluffiest of white heads keeps the soft malts subdued to allow the spicy, lemony aromas and distinctive hop flavours take centre stage, steadily building bitterness to create a dry, refreshing drop.

THE STORY The role of, and respect for, beer as a deserving partner for food in even the finest of dining establishments has changed immeasurably in Australia in recent years. Few are in a better position to have witnessed this change than Stefano de Pieri, the much-awarded chef based in Mildura who has both a range of wines and a microbrewery to his name. Like many of the recipes he designs for his restaurant, the beer that bears his name from the Mildura range is a nod to his forebears in Italy. Based on the classic European pilsner style, it is, of course, a versatile food beer.

Brewer's food match
Linguine with chilli prawns

Availability
Year round

Where to find it
Dan Murphy's Australia-wide, selected Vintage Cellars and First Choice Liquor, selected independent bottle shops; on tap in Melbourne at Mrs Palmas, Transport Bar, Collins Quarter, Trunk, Beaufort, Post Office Hotel, Meatball & Wine Bar, Fitzrovia, Radio Mexico, Local Taphouse, Dan O'Connell's

Brewery and cellar door location
20 Langtree Avenue, Mildura, Victoria

Brewery website
www.mildurabrewery.com.au

Pilsner
MOO BREW

 Pilsner   5.0%   6-8°C  *Tall pilsner glass*

TASTING NOTES Moo Brew's pilsner pours bright golden with a fluffy white head, with a nose that's predominantly spicy with a touch of lemon. There's a touch of honey sweetness to the malt flavour before things are wrapped up nice and dry.

THE STORY Whenever I think of Moo Brew, there is one word that springs to mind more often than any other: tight. Don't expect to find anything flabby in the range. The Dark Ale: tight. The Hefeweizen: tight. Their packaging (indeed, everything about their unique bottles): tight. You get the message. Tasted fresh, the pilsner, brewed with the noble German hop variety Spalt, is as clean, sharp and refreshingly dry as any lager currently being brewed in Australia.

Given Moo Brew is part of the David Walsh empire that also includes MONA, the Museum of Old and New Art, which has exhibited animal carcasses, artwork featuring the imprints of lipstick-coated sphincters, and German-conceived machines that recreate human intestines designed to deposit Mr Whippy–style faeces onto silver platters, it's a wonder that the brewery is associated with such words as 'clean' and 'tight'. But that's how it is, with the pilsner the tightest of the lot.

Brewer's food match
Fish and chips

Availability
Year round

Where to find it
Australia-wide

Brewery location
76A Cove Hill Road, Bridgewater, Tasmania

Cellar door
Museum of Old and New Art (MONA), 655 Main Road, Berriedale, Tasmania

Brewery website
www.moobrew.com.au

Love Tap Double Lager
MOON DOG CRAFT BREWERY

 **Double lager**   5.9%    4-6°C   **Pint**

TASTING NOTES This is a beer that applies the kind of hopping regime usually found in an IPA to a lager, albeit one of a reasonably high alcohol percentage. Use of Old and New World hops allows it to run the gamut from tropical and citrus fruits through spiciness and distinctly herbal flavours to a bitter denouement.

THE STORY They burst onto the Aussie beer scene like creatures from another planet, belching, farting and cussing their way out of a homebuilt spaceship that had veered off course and crash-landed in a country that needed them, but didn't necessarily know it just yet. Two violin-playing brothers and their mate took over an industrial unit midway between CUB's HQ and a brothel in Abbotsford and began brewing beers such as barrel-aged, fruit-infused wild ales and high-octane barley wines, all packaged with the wildest of names and labels.

Eventually, they felt they needed a volume shifter and came up with Love Tap, a highly hopped, high ABV lager that, in its original incarnation, was over 7 per cent and, at its freshest, tasted like drinking thick, juicy hop goo. Toned down a little now, refined and popped inside bottles adorned with a pig wearing a bowtie, Bluetooth headset, mortarboard or monocle (depending which bottle you pick up), it now makes up the vast majority of their output.

Brewer's food match
Pepperoni pizza

Availability
Year round

Where to find it
Australia-wide

Brewery and cellar door location
17 Duke Street, Abbotsford, Victoria

Brewery website
www.moondogbrewing.com.au

Pilsner

RED HILL BREWERY

 Pilsner   5.0%   4°C    Footed pilsner style

TASTING NOTES This delightful pilsner pours a hazy pale yellow with a fluffy white head and draws the drinker in with its appealing lemon, hay and spicy hop aromas. The same characteristics are there in the mouth, alongside some sweet malts, before a distinctive bitterness and dryness washes over the palate in the most refreshing of manners.

THE STORY It was while holidaying in the UK, enjoying the country's wonderful old pubs and real ales, that the seeds of the idea that would become Red Hill Brewery were sown in the minds of Karen and David Golding. Yet, while their regular range of beers and long list of seasonals are peppered with British styles, they have never been afraid to plunder the rest of Europe for inspiration either. They brew a German- style Hefeweizen; a beer based on a Kolsch; a strong, dark wheat beer (seen elsewhere in this book); as well as multiple Belgian-inspired beers. Up until 2012, they also released a Bohemian pilsner annually, based on beers David had enjoyed while drinking with fellow brewers in New Zealand. A delicious, creamy, spicy affair, it was removed from their annual schedule in 2012 to be replaced with a lighter-bodied, lower-ABV pilsner that would be sold year round. Any temptation to bemoan the loss of their fine and much-anticipated annual release soon dissipated, with the new beer turning out to be one of the finest craft lagers to come out of Australia.

Brewer's food match
Goat's cheese

Availability
Year round

Where to find it
Quality bottle shops and bars in Victoria, New South Wales and Queensland

Brewery and cellar door location
88 Shoreham Road, Red Hill South, Victoria

Brewery website
www.redhillbrewery.com.au

Pilsner
THE AUSTRALIAN BREWERY

 Pilsner  4.8% 4-6°C Pilsner flute

TASTING NOTES While their Mexican lager caters for the Corona crowds, this is the Australian Brewery's lager for the more discerning drinker. Lemon, citrus and spicy hop aromas kick off this re-creation of a Czech-style pilsner with spicy and herbal hop flavours followed by a firm, dry and refreshing bitterness.

THE STORY It takes more than a little self-belief to decide to open a brewery in 2010 and give it the name 'The Australian Brewery'. That said, opening a microbrewery in the far-from-crafty northwestern Sydney suburb of Rouse Hill doesn't exactly hint at lack of confidence either. A steadily growing nationwide distribution, not to mention contracts to send their canned beers to international markets, suggests such confidence was well founded. Head brewer Neal Cameron, who is also a respected beer judge and beer writer, has created a range that mixes beers aimed fairly and squarely at the brewery's local market with others, usually seasonal releases, with more discerning palates in mind. The Pilsner should appeal to both, not least because it's one of the finest lagers you'll find in Australia.

Brewer's food match
Tempura flathead with hand-cut chips

Availability
Year round

Where to find it
Australia-wide at Dan Murphy's, independent bottle shops around Sydney and Canberra

Brewery and cellar door location
350 Annangrove Road, Rouse Hill, New South Wales

Brewery website
www.australianbrewery.com.au

Keller Instinct

WAYWARD BREWING COMPANY

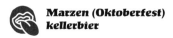 Marzen (Oktoberfest) kellerbier   5.0%   4°C   Tulip glass

TASTING NOTES This twist on the kellerbier style pours a vibrant rusty colour with floral, spicy noble hop aromas soon subsumed by the sweet, spicy malts that prepare you for a relatively full-bodied, slick beer with rich biscuit and spice malt flavours, a soft bitterness and a distinctly dry finish that lingers on the palate.

THE STORY Wayward Brewing Company may have launched with the New World–inspired Charmer India Red Ale, but gypsy brewer Peter Philip has followed it with a series of beers that take their lead from Europe. Frequently these take the lead from less-common beers, or are delivered in a rather unique interpretation. There has been an eisbock, a rich, dessert-like, high-ABV beer that involves partial freezing during the production process; an authentic Biere de Garde, a French/Belgian traditional farmhouse ale; and a spiced saison.

Then there is the punny Keller Instinct, which looks to the generally hoppier, richer lager beers that originate in the Franconia region of southern Germany, then adds rye malt to give it an even fuller body and a touch of extra spice to boot.

Brewer's food match
Pulled pork tacos or pizza with spicy sausage

Availability
Year round

Where to find it
Limited bottle supply, good availability on draught at craft beer establishments in Sydney, occasionally available in Melbourne and Brisbane; Harts Pub, The Australian Hotel, The Wild Rover, The

Pumphouse, Spooning Goats, The Empire Hotel, Chippendale Hotel, Forest Lodge Hotel

Brewery location
Gypsy brewed

Cellar door
Batch Brewing Co, 44 Sydenham Road, Marrickville, New South Wales

Brewery website
www.waywardbrewing.com.au

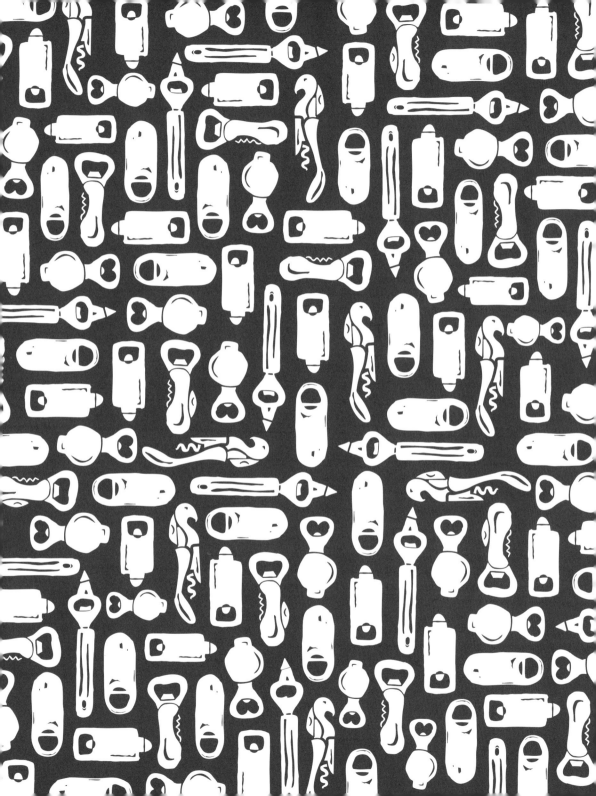

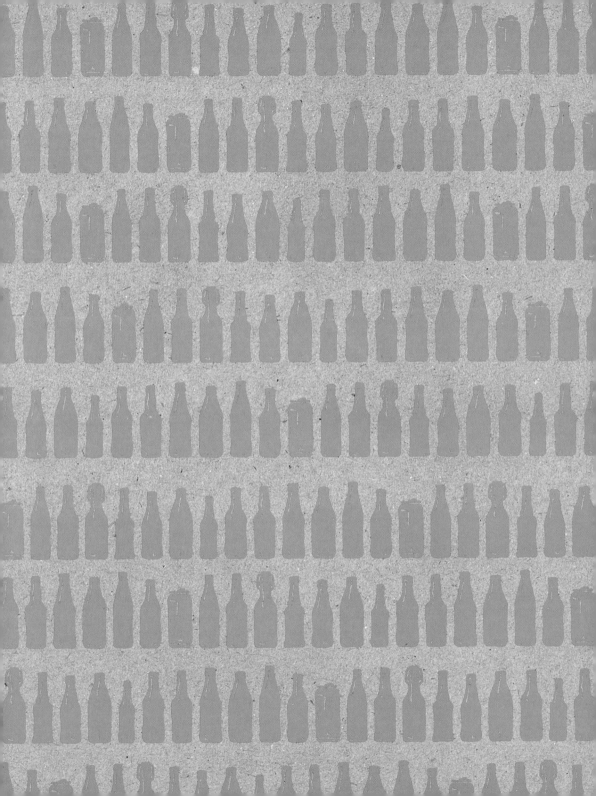

Session Ales

Beer is a wonderfully subjective thing. Put a group of experienced brewers together at a table and ask them to judge a series of beers against strict style guidelines and you would expect them to come up with similar results. Give the same group of brewers the same series of beers and ask them which ones they *like* the best and, chances are, you would get very different results.

People's tastes differ. There will be those for whom a balanced IPA will be their choice when sitting down for the proverbial 'session'. The same beer would prove challenging for many other drinkers.

For the purposes of this collection of 'session ales', the peccadilloes of the more extreme or adventurous drinkers are ignored in favour of beers that the vast majority would consider sessionable: mid-strengths and approachable, light-coloured ales that might be tagged 'golden ales' or 'summer ales' or referred to as 'gateway' beers: those that offer newcomers to the world of craft beer a gentle introduction as they move away from generic lagers.

Mid-strength as a category is self-explanatory: typically beers around 3.5 per cent ABV. It is one that is becoming more diverse and heavily populated in Australia. For years, drinkers looking for a fuller flavoured mid-strength had little other than Rogers from Little Creatures on offer. Today, while that beer remains a classic of its kind, it has been joined by a growing number from brewers looking to achieve the dual aims of lower alcohol content and higher flavour.

There are 'tiny IPAs', which look to create beers with imposing hop aromatics and high bitterness at low alcohol levels; beers inspired by English milds that are typically malt-driven; as well as reduced-alcohol German-style lagers. Many from Australian microbreweries are still at the development stage or draught-only releases, but expect more to be packaged in the coming years.

It is a different story entirely when it comes to golden ales. The biggest growth within the craft sector, despite the hype that surrounds IPAs or each winter's batch of imperial stouts, belongs to pale and golden ales around the 4.5 per cent ABV mark. In the past year or two, it seems almost every brewery without a golden ale on the roster has added one. Whether it's down to the phenomenal success of Stone & Wood's Pacific Ale or the desire to try and capture the growing number of people taking their first steps outside the mainstream, 'golden' or 'summer' ales are nigh on ubiquitous.

So what should drinkers expect from such beers? Aside from being golden in colour (or, often in the case of summer ales, a lighter shade of yellow), they are beers in which malt character is restrained to the extent that the brewer's choice of hops can take centre stage, although with the focus on capturing hop aroma without significant bitterness. That said, there are golden ales out there in which hop character is also restrained, although none that make this book. (Surely a beer should have *some* character...) Golden ales should finish dry too, something that is often achieved through the use of wheat malt, with dryness lending them much of their refreshing character.

Golden ales of a British bent will tend to have a more floral hop aroma, while the vast majority of those brewed locally favour New World hop varieties, so expect more citrusy or tropical fruit characteristics, as evidenced by the cream of the crop, Stone & Wood's tropical fruit salad explosion, the Pacific Ale.

TOP OF THE HOPS

STONE & WOOD PACIFIC ALE
BONEYARD BREWING GOLDEN ALE
NAIL BREWING GOLDEN NAIL

Golden Ale
BONEYARD BREWING

 Aggressively hopped golden ale   **4.5%**  **4-6°C**   **IPA glass**

TASTING NOTES This is a beer that nudges the upper realms of the golden ale style, but is none the worse for it. Exploding with zesty aromatics, the malt is there to do little more than allow the citrusy, grapefruit-like hops shine before bringing the curtain down with a resoundingly dry flourish.

THE STORY Brendan O'Sullivan was well known in beer circles as a home brewer of some repute and an astute judge of good beer. Chris Badenoch was even better known as the guy in the hat who'd brought cooking with beer into the national consciousness when he appeared on Australian *Masterchef*. When the former took up the role of beer sommelier at the latter's now defunct Josie Bones restaurant in Melbourne, it was inevitable that their coming together would lead to a beery spin-off.

In 2012 it did, with the launch of Boneyard Brewing, a brewery-hopping venture that sees Brendan and Chris – and occasionally their friends from the beer world – conceive beers that they believe are missing from the Australian palette, frequently designed with the dining table in mind. This was their first, a golden ale that pushes the upper reaches of that style in terms of hop character and bitterness, with the result a super-aromatic, super-dry and refreshing ale.

Brewer's food match
Mussels in spicy coconut curry sauce; Singapore black pepper crab; paprika-dusted school prawns; cauliflower pakora

Availability
Year round

Where to find it
Good bottle shops, bars and restaurants around Australia; wholesale via Northdown Craft Beer Movement

Brewery and cellar door location
6 Fogarty Street, North Melbourne, Victoria

Brewery website
www.boneyardbrewing.com.au

Red Ale

BONEYARD BREWING

 Mild session ale 2.9% 8-10°C Pint

TASTING NOTES This mid-strength ale pours a russet red in colour with an off-white head. Aromas of nuts and sweet orange lead into a palate that mixes biscuity and caramel malts with some solid piny hop characters in a full-flavoured beer that belies its alcohol content.

THE STORY Having focused firmly on the realm of hops for their first two beers, the golden ale (see previous entry) and a grapefruit IPA that uses actual grapefruit zest in the brew, Boneyard Brewing changed direction for beer number three.

Inspired initially by customer requests for a full-flavoured mid-strength at co-founder Chris Badenoch's old restaurant, Josie Bones, and then stylistically by a combination of American amber ales and English milds, this red ale confirmed home brewer–turned–pro brewer Brendan O'Sullivan as one to watch. There has been a rising tide of Australian brewers looking to create lower-alcohol beers with enough character to satisfy demanding drinkers; few have achieved a result to top this.

Brewer's food match
Hanger steak with bone marrow and chimichurri

Availability
Year round

Where to find it
Good bottle shops, bars and restaurants around Australia; wholesale via Northdown Craft Beer Movement

Brewery and cellar door location
6 Fogarty Street, North Melbourne, Victoria

Brewery website
www.boneyardbrewing.com.au

Rogers

LITTLE CREATURES BREWING

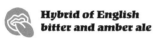 **Hybrid of English bitter and amber ale** **3.8%** **4.8-5°C** **Pint glass**

TASTING NOTES Just as you would expect in a beer from Little Creatures, this is all about the balance. It's a bright amber ale with a gentle floral and spicy hop aroma, backed up with a touch of toffee. It's light on the palate, where citrusy fruits meld with slightly toasted and nutty flavours in a beer that's more flavoursome than it has any right to be.

THE STORY With the global beer world experiencing an era of unprecedented innovation and creativity, it seems barely a week goes by without a new beer style being invented, or two, maybe three, styles being shoehorned into one class. Trends come and trends go, sometimes just as fast.

But among all of the recent trends, one that seems to be steadily gathering momentum, rather than doing an Icarus, is the development of full-flavoured mid-strength beers. For years, Rogers has

been the benchmark in this field: a beer inspired by classic English ales that offers plenty in the way of malt character with some appealing hop aromatics dancing on top, too. Its name pays tribute to a pair of legends of the Australian beer world, Roger Bailey and Roger Bussell.

Availability
Year round

Where to find it
Available at all good bottle shops Australia-wide

Brewery and cellar door locations
40 Mews Road, Fremantle, Western Australia; Cnr Fyans and Swanston streets, Geelong, Victoria

Brewery website
www.littlecreatures.com.au

Grasscutter
MASH BREWING

 Summer ale 4.4% 6-8°C Pint

TASTING NOTES Mash's brewery is situated in the Swan Valley wine region, and this beer has much in common with wine. The aromatics rising from this clear, straw-coloured beer are subtle peach and oak, while on the palate it is creamy and gently fruity, but also possesses an oaky dryness.

THE STORY In its own way, this beer is one of the quirkiest you'll find in this book. At just 4.4 per cent and pitched unashamedly as a session – or, more specifically, lawnmower – beer, it nevertheless could have just as easily landed a spot in the specialty section as here alongside the other session ales. The Grasscutter is part of Mash's Illustrated Ales series, beers for which they commission a different artist to design the label.

The artwork is far from the only creative element of the beer. It is fermented on two different toasts of French oak, which lends it characteristics more commonly found in the white wines produced in the Swan Valley. The process is clearly handled with kid gloves, as it's one that could have left such a delicate base beer tasting like splinters, but instead leaves the drinker contemplating an intriguing and complex quaffer.

Brewer's food match
Crispy Szechuan calamari; beer-battered pearl snapper

Availability
Year round

Where to find it
The Quarie, Liquor Barons Bayswater and Morley, and other selected bottle shops in Perth

Brewery and cellar door location
10250 West Swan Road, Henley Brook, Swan Valley, Western Australia

Brewery website
www.mashbrewing.com

Summer Ale

MOUNTAIN GOAT

 Summer ale   4.7%  3°C   Tulip glass

TASTING NOTES Based on the Skipping Girl beer that Mountain Goat released in draught form over a few summers, but softened for broader appeal, this beer has been likened to Passiona thanks to its dominant tropical Kiwi hop aromas and flavours. Bitterness is minimal, with lashings of wheat giving it a dry, freshening finish.

THE STORY Melbourne's Mountain Goat wasn't the first Australian microbrewery to put beer into cans. That honour goes to The Australian Brewery in New South Wales. But it was Mountain Goat's Summer Ale that saw craft in cans really capture the public's attention. With no canning line of their own, the beer was brewed under licence at a facility that demanded a sizeable minimum run. As such, they ordered just one run to assess the market's readiness for such a venture. Within a week of the first cans hitting shelves, they placed an order for a second run; a third followed soon afterwards.

In fact, having been inspired to put a beer in cans partly so the brewers themselves could take them to Victoria's summer music festivals, the initial surge meant bottle shop shelves were only just restocked in time for the festival season. With a growing number of advocates for the benefits of cans, and fellow Victorians Mornington Peninsula Brewery installing their own canning line, festivalgoers can look forward to bidding the days of slabs of imported Euro lagers goodbye.

Brewer's food match
Salt and pepper calamari

Availability
Seasonal (summer)

Where to find it
Australia-wide

Brewery and cellar door location
80 North Street, Richmond, Victoria

Brewery website
www.goatbeer.com.au

Golden Nail

NAIL BREWING

 English summer ale   5.0%   4°C   *Pint glass*

TASTING NOTES This is a golden ale that does well to add 'hoppy summer ale' to the label, given its much stronger personality than many beers bearing that tag in Australia. It looks like a cloudy golden sunset, has a lovely, clean tropical fruit aroma and a full, almost sticky palate that mixes sweet malts and resinous, grapefruity bitterness.

THE STORY During an early encounter I had with Nail Brewing's John Stallwood, he declared that he was 'a pale ale and stout brewer'. For the most part, since launching Nail Brewing more than a decade ago, he has stayed true to that. There has been Nail Ale, an excellent Australian pale ale for which he had registered a trademark five years before entering the world of commercial brewing, and low-alcohol lighter versions

of it. Then there is an oatmeal stout and imperial stout (both found elsewhere in this book) to bolster his claim.

More recently, however, he has deviated a little from the norm. There have been brown ales (standard and imperial), as well as this 'hoppy summer ale'. Proof that golden ales can have plenty of character and more than a little bite, it is a welcome addition to the lineup of one of Australia's most consistent brewers – one whose beers will hopefully be reaching far more drinkers in the coming years.

Brewer's food match
To be enjoyed on a desert island

Availability
Year round

Where to find it
Australia-wide

Brewery location
Bassendean, Western Australia

Brewery website
www.nailbrewing.com.au

1851

RED DUCK BREWERY

 Golden ale 4.7% Icy cold Your favourite

TASTING NOTES A hazy, golden ale with a fluffy, long-lasting white head. The hops take the form of peach and kiwifruit alongside some soft, sweet malts in a beer with a pillowy mouthfeel and bitterness that tidies up loose ends without outstaying its welcome.

THE STORY Among the rather manic twists and turns that make up a rollercoaster of a release schedule from Ballarat's Red Duck – including smoky medieval stouts, mouth-puckering sours and Egyptian bread beers (see elsewhere in this book) – there are occasional moments of sanity. In fact, one of the beers that stood out among the brewery's kaleidoscopic and pun-laden roster in 2013 was one called, simply, 'Topaz'.

The beer was as simple as its name: it featured a single malt and a single hop variety (Australia's Topaz). And it was delicious, proof that, when not trying to outdo himself with another flight of fantasy, Scott Wilson-Browne can brew a straight-down-the-line beer too.

It's an approach he brought to one of the most recent additions to his permanent range, the 1851, a golden that takes its name from the year gold was first discovered in Ballarat. This time, the single hop is New Zealand's Nelson Sauvin and, in a style category that can tend towards the bland, it is both sessionable and characterful.

Brewer's food match
Flathead fillets in panko bread crumbs or deep-fried tofu with peanut sauce

Availability
Year round

Where to find it
Good boutique bottle shops, bars and restaurants

Brewery location
Ballarat

Cellar door
11A Michaels Drive, Alfredton, Victoria

Brewery website
www.redduckbeer.com.au

Garden Ale
STONE & WOOD

 English bitter **3.8%** **3.5°C** **Pint**

TASTING NOTES The revised 2014 version of this beer offers up grassy, spicy and herbal hops on the nose, thanks to the use of relatively new Australian hop variety Ella. On the palate, berries – particularly strawberries – are added to the mix, with the soft crystal malts playing a supporting role.

THE STORY While not every microbrewer or craft beer fanatic will agree, balance is an essential element in any great beer. It is something you will find the many winemakers who have turned to brewing (and there are plenty of them in Australia) advocating more than anything else. The wine-to-beer route is one that Stone & Wood's head brewer Brad Rogers took, and you will find them striving for perfect balance in everything they brew. It is a key factor in enticing the drinker back for more, and thus a key factor in a beer such as their annual summer release, the Garden Ale.

Inspired by the sort of sessionable ales quaffed in English beer gardens on those rare English summer days, it just so happens to be the sort of sessionable ale you'd want to quaff all day in a beer garden on one of Australia's many hot summer days.

Brewer's food match
Slab of aged cheddar

Availability
Seasonal (summer)

Where to find it
Good bars and bottle shops
Australia-wide

Brewery and cellar door location
4 Boronia Place, Byron Bay,
New South Wales

Brewery website
www.stoneandwood.com.au

Pacific Ale
STONE & WOOD

 English summer ale 4.4% 4°C *Schooner or pilsner glass*

TASTING NOTES Galaxy is the star of the Australian hop-breeding program, and no beer showcases its distinct passionfruit and citrus character better than this cloudy, pale golden ale that backs up its big hop aromas with similarly tropical flavours. It finishes nice and dry, perfect for the end of a hot day in Byron Bay, where it was conceived.

THE STORY What's left to be said about this beer that has taken Australia by storm? Launched as Draught Ale and intended for the Byron Bay brewery's local market, word spread, the beer was bottled, and a phenomenon was born. It's a phenomenon that has required the building of a major new brewery and

spawned a host of imitators. Yet it's also a phenomenon that was carefully plotted.

Stone & Wood was formed by three mates with decades of experience within the craft arm of a major brewery, who understood how to build a brand. Before launching their brewery, they sat down with dozens of beers from around the world, analysing what they liked and didn't like in each in minute detail to come up with what they believed would be the perfect beer. A few trial batches at head brewer Brad Rogers' home, and what would become Pacific Ale was born. Whether they knew just how well it would be received, well ...

Brewer's food match
A fresh, light dish like chilled prawns with mango chilli jam

Availability
Year round

Where to find it
Selected bottle shops, restaurants and bars; see website for full list of stockists

Brewery and cellar door location
4 Boronia Place, Byron Bay, New South Wales

Brewery website
www.stoneandwood.com.au

Bicycle Beer

TEMPLE BREWING COMPANY

 **American wheat** **4.2%**  **4-6°C** **Pot glass**

TASTING NOTES Given its home is in East Brunswick, this quaffer could well have been called 'The Fixie'. It features a blend of seven different hops that create a subtle citrus aroma atop a beer characterised by soft malts and a dry finish enhanced by the use of an ancient sea salt from the Grampians.

THE STORY Having garnered a reputation for making some of the finest beers in Australia while brewing on other people's gear, just before Christmas 2011, Temple Brewing Company opened a unique brewery and contemporary, industrial-chic brasserie and bar in Melbourne's East Brunswick. A series of cracking beers followed, but so did a turbulent ride that saw ownership change and some founding members leave.

Whether would-be Aussie icons like the astounding Midnight IPA or the much-loved Saison will return remains to be seen, but this light, hoppy, dry session ale that was launched when they opened their brewery has wasted little time finding favour well beyond Temple's East Brunswick home.

Brewer's food match
Hand-made pretzels with hop salt and crispy fried chicken

Availability
Year round ·

Where to find it
Australia-wide

Brewery and cellar door location
122 Weston Street, Brunswick East, Victoria

Brewery website
www.templebrewing.com.au

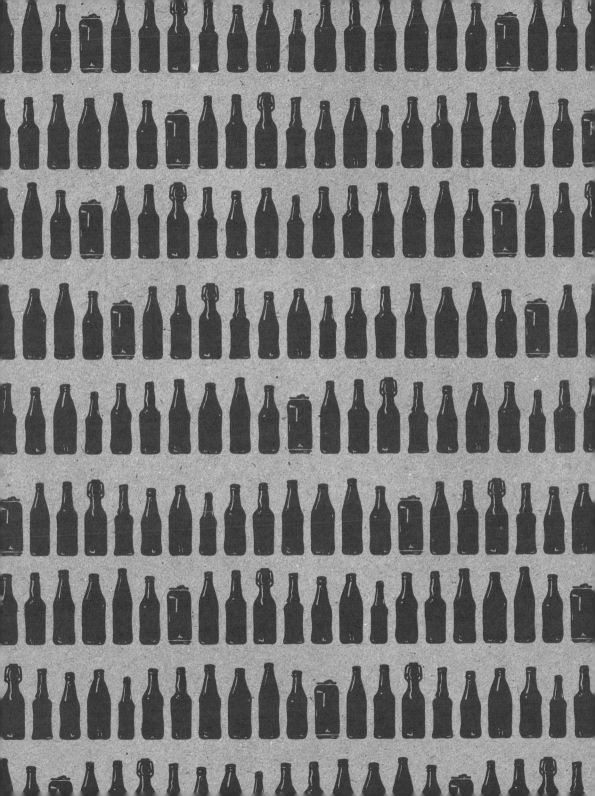

PALE
ALES

Pale Ales

Take a journey back through beer's history and the first pale ales are generally acknowledged to have come out of breweries in Burton upon Trent in the UK. Yet this chapter could just as easily be entitled 'American Pale Ales'.

As with many traditional styles, the humble English pale ale has been picked up by the brewers of the American craft-beer revolution, pumped full of steroids, sent to the gym with its own personal trainer, and had its tweed suit, monocle and pipe replaced with sunnies and board shorts, and its soundtrack of *Greensleeves* replaced by fat beats and an even fatter blunt.

American brewers' bolder, more hop-forward take on the style, embellished by the punchily aromatic hops of the Pacific Northwest, was first introduced in the states in the form of Anchor Steam's Liberty Ale, then popularised further by the pale ale from fellow Californians Sierra Nevada.

Later, in the same way that those beers changed a generation's drinking habits in the US, Little Creatures Pale Ale did the same for Australia. The beer that brought American hops and the American pale ale style to Australia around the turn of the millennium has sparked countless imitators, with good reason: for almost every Australian microbrewery that has an American-inspired pale ale on its roster, it is their bestselling beer.

That said, you can find a handful of English-style pales in Australia (there are some in the chapter on British and Irish styles) and a tiny number of Belgian-style pales (less hops, more yeast-derived fruitiness). Then there is the Australian pale ale.

Essentially created by Coopers Sparkling (see British & Irish Ales) and Pale, the Australian pale ale used to share more in common with the English pale ales upon which it was modelled in early colonial days, due to its fruity yeast characteristics and relatively subdued hop aroma. There are beers of a more recent vintage that follow in Coopers' footsteps, notably Nail Brewing's multiple trophy-winning Nail Ale, but, more often than not, contemporary Australian pale ales tend to share more characteristics with those from the US.

What that means in practice is beers that are golden or amber in colour often hazy or cloudy, too. This can be due to craft brewers leaving their beer unfiltered as a nod to tradition, or even as a visible point of difference from the crystal-clear beers from their multinational counterparts. Some microbreweries will bottle-condition their beers as well – in other words, keep active yeast still in the bottled product – and the yeast's presence also adds a hazy appearance.

Depending on the origin of the hops, you should expect citrus, stone fruit, pine, tropical or grassy aromas. It is worth remembering that these hop aromas and flavours disappear fastest from a beer, hence why these beers should be enjoyed as fresh as possible.

While hop characteristics are key with these beers, they are nothing without balance. Typically, malt flavours will be of a biscuity, toasty or caramel nature, but generally they are there to play a supporting role to the fruity hop flavours in beers that finish relatively dry with a firm bitterness.

TOP OF THE HOPS

MATILDA BAY BREWING COMPANY ALPHA PALE ALE
HOLGATE BREWHOUSE MT MACEDON PALE ALE
4 PINES BREWING COMPANY PALE ALE

Pale Ale

4 PINES BREWING COMPANY

 American-style pale ale **5.4%** **4-6°C**  **Pint**

TASTING NOTES This beer is at the upper end of the colour range for pales, pouring a bright amber, and doesn't hold back anywhere else either. Prominent citrus and pine aromas combine with rich toffee malts in a beer with a solid bitterness to close things out.

THE STORY Now armed with two breweries – their original 500-litre brewpub setup overlooking the Manly ferry terminal and their main production brewery ten times its size in Brookvale – the ever-expanding brewing team at 4 Pines is responsible for around thirty different beers each year. Yet if such diversity could be thought to pose a threat to the consistency and quality of their core range, think again. Nowhere is this better displayed than with their Pale Ale.

In one sense, it is a beer that has little to make it stand out from the crowd: it's their approximation of a hoppy American pale ale. What sets it apart from the rest, however, is just how good an approximation of that style it is, with its alluring hops sitting in perfect harmony with its malt backbone. That they've hit upon a winning formula has been borne out whenever I've placed it in a blind tasting; whether private or public, rated by beer lovers or experienced brewers, it always rates highly.

Brewer's food match
Red meats, hotter chilli and spice flavours, strong vintage cheddar or blue cheese

Availability
Year round

Where to find it
National retailers, good independents and on tap at selected venues

Brewery location
4F, 9–13 Winbourne Road, Brookvale, New South Wales

Cellar door
29/43-45 E Esplanade, Manly, New South Wales

Brewery website
www.4pinesbeer.com.au

Alpha Queen

BOATROCKER BREWING COMPANY

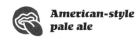 **American-style pale ale**   **5.0%**  **4-7°C**   **Pint glass**

TASTING NOTES Steadily refined since Boatrocker opened its own brewery – and increasingly late-hopped in its custom-designed hopback too – this kicks off with appealing citrus and tropical fruit aromas backed up by some spiciness that sits alongside the toffee malt backbone. A cleansing bitterness makes for a balanced and eminently sessionable New World pale ale.

THE STORY It will be interesting to watch the development of Boatrocker now that it operates its own brewery. Early signs are that it will allow co-owner Matt Houghton to explore his fascination with Belgian and barrel-aged beers, a far cry from the more straightforward beers with which the brewing company made its name while having beer brewed under licence. Early successes included Hoppbier, a gold medal–winning New World take on Northern German pilsners, and debut release Alpha Queen.

This beer may now reside in the rather overpopulated 'hoppy US-inspired pale ale' category but, six years ago, it was a pretty bold opening salvo with its punchy hop aroma and solid British backbone. And, following a few tweaks since production was moved in-house, it remains one of the tastiest. With an experimental hop farm planted in country Victoria at which Matt plans to develop his own varieties, look out for Boatrocker continuing to plough the hoppy furrow that announced it to the world.

Brewer's food match
Spicy lamb koftas with goat's cheese and rocket salad

Availability
Year round

Where to find it
Australia-wide at good craft bottle shops, and on tap at good craft beer pubs

Brewery and cellar door location
51 Macbeth Street, Braeside, Victoria

Brewery website
www.boatrocker.com.au

Hop Zone Session IPA
BREWCULT

 Session IPA 5.0% 6°C **Spiegelau IPA glass or shaker pint**

TASTING NOTES Session IPA or hopped-up pale ale? I'm opting for the latter here, with this year-round release from Victoria's BrewCult a riot of citrus and tropical fruit aromas with just about enough of a malt backbone to keep its overt hoppiness from running wild.

THE STORY The beer world is full of characters, few of them as colourful as Steve 'Hendo' Henderson. Having come to the brewing game fairly late in life, he wasted little time tailoring his own unique path through it. After learning the ropes at Prickly Moses in the Otway Ranges, there followed a short spell at Southern Bay, on Victoria's south coast, before he embarked on his own journey as BrewCult. The Hop Zone is easily the sanest of the beers he's since released,

brewed on his friends' gear at Cavalier in Melbourne's west.

Who knows what you might find bearing the BrewCult logo? Within his first year of operation, Hendo had under his belt beers that amalgamated Belgian and American styles, releases bearing 70s-style psychedelic labels with names such as 'Don't Fight the Funk' and, perhaps most memorably, 'Acid Freaks'. Hendo's older brother is a maker of artisan vinegars in Queensland. So, inspired by the growing popularity of sour beers, the two got together to create something that combined their two passions. The result was a Balsamic Porter, a rich, chocolatey dark beer brewed with a percentage of barrel-aged balsamic vinegar. Go figure ...

- -

Brewer's food match
Buffalo wings

Availability
Year round

Where to find it
All good specialty craft beer bottle shops and selected hotels and pubs

across Australia, but mainly New South Wales, Queensland and Victoria

Brewery location
Derrimut, Victoria

Brewery website
www.brewcult.com

- -

Beechworth Pale Ale

BRIDGE ROAD BREWERS

 New World pale ale   **4.8%**   **4–8°C**    **IPA glass**

TASTING NOTES Bridge Road's flagship beer is this American pale ale brewed with New World hops to create an ale dominated by citrus and tropical fruit aromas and flavours, yet nicely balanced and finishing refreshingly dry and lean.

THE STORY Today, he is one of the most respected brewers in Australia, as well as one of the best-known Aussies overseas, thanks to his multiple collaborations with international brewers. But in his early twenties, Ben Kraus intended to be a winemaker. A fact-finding mission to Europe somehow ended up with him working at an Austrian brewery instead, and he returned to his home in Beechworth as a brewer.

Initially, Bridge Road Brewers operated out of a shed owned by Kraus's parents (now converted into accommodation, should you wish to sleep where beer was once brewed) before shifting to the Old Coach House in the centre of town. This pale ale, Kraus's bestselling beer, was given the name of its hometown, presumably in the hope that it would bring attention to the beer in the brewery's earliest days. Things have turned full circle now, with Bridge Road Brewers one of Beechworth's main attractions, enticing tourists, beer lovers, families and locals in equal measure to sample a wide range of beers alongside traditional pretzels and colourful pizzas amid an ever-expanding sea of stainless steel brewing equipment.

Brewer's food match
Slightly spicy Middle Eastern dishes

Availability
Year round

Where to find it
Australia-wide

Brewery and cellar door location
50 Ford Street, Beechworth, Victoria

Brewery website
www.bridgeroadbrewers.com.au

Blowhard Pale Ale

BRIGHT BREWERY

 American pale ale    5.0%   5-6°C   Tulip glass

TASTING NOTES Since its recent reinvention, Bright's Blowhard Pale Ale has become one of the finest locally brewed examples of an American-style pale ale. Its powerful citrus aromas follow through into an almost resinous mouthfeel, with real depth to the hop flavours and a nice, cleansing bitterness.

THE STORY Brewer Jon Seltin's decision to go paragliding over the mountains of Victoria's High Country on the day he was supposed to be kegging off a brand-new beer, then driving it to Melbourne to be launched at a showcase, was probably not the best way of ingratiating himself with his new bosses. He lost control and was forced to crash land, and had no means of contacting his colleagues. A search and rescue party was sent out and, ten hours after he was due back originally, he walked into the brewery, made his excuses and set about kegging the aforementioned beer.

It had been a beer without a name, but was instantly named the MIA IPA in honour of his exploits. It was also a wonderfully aromatic, perfectly poised take on the style that first notified the Aussie beer world that this was a brewer to watch. The beer still appears on tap once or twice a year, but for an insight into what it delivers, drinkers can hunt down the Blowhard Pale Ale from Bright's year-round range. A reinvention of one of the brewery's initial beers, it captures much of the wonderful hop aromas and flavours of the IPA but in a smaller, more tightly packaged form.

Brewer's food match
Complements cheese, smoked meat, nut and fruit platters; contrasts with spicy salsas and curries

Availability
Year round

Where to find it
Specialist bottle shops in Victoria

Brewery and cellar door location
121 Great Alpine Road, Bright, Victoria

Brewery website
www.brightbrewery.com.au

28 Pale Ale
BURLEIGH BREWING

 American pale ale   **4.8%**    **6°C**   **American pint glass**

TASTING NOTES With floral and citrus aromas up front, the 28 pours a bright copper, with some sweet caramel malts and a bitter tang with hints of orange marmalade, grapefruit and lychee, all rounded off with a gentle zing at the end.

THE STORY If any brewer in Australia should know how to knock out a quality American pale ale, it's Brennan Fielding, the globe-trotting Hawaiian who founded Burleigh Brewing with wife, Peta, on the Gold Coast. With an enviable brewing pedigree behind him before making the move to Australia, he has continued to add gongs with regularity ever since.

It's not just smarts in the recipe development and brewing side of the business that he brings, either. While countless breweries across Australia open, realise they underestimated, hit capacity, expand, hit capacity, expand again, wish they'd bought a bigger brewery in the first place, hit capacity, and so on, Burleigh started out with an operation that still dwarfs most micros in the country. That said, they are growing too, steadily taking over unit after unit after unit in their corner of Burleigh Heads with an appetite bordering on the insatiable.

Brewer's food match
Moroccan lamb

Availability
Year round

Where to find it
Distribution focused in southeast Queensland, but available Australia-wide in selected liquor chains, independent

bottle shops and a variety of bars and restaurants

Brewery and cellar door location
17A Ern Harley Drive, Burleigh Heads, Queensland

Brewery website
www.burleighbrewing.com.au

Pale Ale

CAVALIER BREWING

 New World pale ale   5.0%  6°C   Stemmed tulip glass

TASTING NOTES Cavalier's biggest seller is typical of the brewery: big and bold. It's packed with New World hops, balanced with a full-bodied malt backbone, and delivers resiny tropical hop flavours, caramel malts and a bitter finish that pulls no punches.

THE STORY It was a chance meeting in a Brunswick dog park that led to the birth of Cavalier Brewing. A home brewer got chatting to a beer lover as they walked their respective pets. The latter, who worked in marketing, rather liked the former's tipples and soon discussions began about taking the brewing from a home environment to a commercial setup. That said, when Cavalier poured its first beers, the threesome was still doing it at home – at the marketing guy's home, to be precise. Their first batches were produced on a 100-litre system in a shed in his Pascoe Vale backyard; before long, they were seeking other breweries who would loan them space before, in 2013, they opened their own facility in Melbourne's west.

Their rapid ascent was made possible by a series of full-flavoured, traditionally minded beers – as well as an enthusiastic showing at countless public events, and marketing guy Heath's self-proclaimed ability to 'sell the proverbial ice to Eskimos'. Their American-inspired pale ale is their biggest mover, as typically robust as every release bearing the Cavalier name.

Brewer's food match
Steamed mussels with chorizo, onion, white wine and garlic sauce topped with fresh coriander

Availability
Year round

Where to find it
Leading craft beer venues Australia-wide

Brewery location
Derrimut, Melbourne, Victoria

Brewery website
www.cavalierbeer.com.au

Pale Ale
EAGLE BAY BREWING

 **American pale ale**   **5.1%**   **4-6°C**   **IPA glass**

TASTING NOTES Having honed his brewing skills from the east coast to the west, Nick d'Espeissis knows what is required to create a solid contemporary pale ale, in which fruity, piny hops sit in harmony with caramel malts.

THE STORY Western Australia's southwest region is home to some of the most spectacular wineries in the country. Increasingly, it doesn't fare too badly on the brewery front either, with the relatively humble early grain-based settlers being joined in recent years by some rather more spectacular ventures.

None fit the 'spectacular' bill better than Eagle Bay Brewing, founded by three siblings on hilltop farming land owned by their parents. The imposing, contemporary building housing their brewery, bar and restaurant peers out over the ocean on the Margaret River's most north-westerly tip, where Nick d'Espeissis brews an ever-improving and ever more creative range of beers. Were it bottled, his ESB would appear here; until it is, the pick of the Eagle Bay packaged range is this American-inspired, hop-forward pale.

Brewer's food match
Eagle Bay Brewing's beef burger

Availability
Year round

Where to find it
A range of bottle shops in Western Australia

Brewery and cellar door location
252 Eagle Bay Road, Eagle Bay, Western Australia

Brewery website
www.eaglebaybrewing.com.au

Mt Macedon Pale Ale

HOLGATE BREWHOUSE

 New World pale ale   **4.5%**   **4-6°C**   **Tulip glass**

TASTING NOTES This is one of Holgate's original beers that has been endlessly honed and refined to become a wonderfully sessionable and refreshingly lean blend of aromatic New World hops and caramel malts.

THE STORY When Paul Holgate launched his brewery from the back of his house in 1999, he was inspired by the pale ales of Europe to offer Australians something better than their usual everyday fare. This beer, a mainstay of the Holgate range since the very early days, started out as a nod to these pale ales.

It is a beer that has evolved, much like the broader Australian craft beer industry. In recent years, it has become cleaner and leaner, its hop aromatics have been tweaked and it has been turned into one of the most consistent session beers on offer from our homegrown brewers. It's the sort of beer that, served in an old-school pint pot with a handle, can transport you in an instant to an English pub beer garden – a feeling that Paul probably always wanted to conjure with the beer, right from the start.

Brewer's food match
Mediterranean-style and tomato-based dishes; home-style herb-based pizza and pasta

Availability
Year round

Where to find it
Australia-wide; check website for full list of stockists

Brewery and cellar door location
79 High Street, Woodend, Victoria

Brewery website
www.holgatebrewhouse.com

Wicked Elf Pale Ale
THE LITTLE BREWING COMPANY

 American pale ale   **5.4%**  **5°C**   **IPA glass**

TASTING NOTES One of the beefiest American-inspired pale ales on the Aussie market, this deep amber beer kicks off with big floral aromas from the use of American Cascade hops, and packs in plenty of toffee and caramel flavours, as well as a relatively high level of booze for the style.

THE STORY Since 2007, The Little Brewing Company has been producing some of the best brewed, most stylistically true and consistent beers in Australia. It has picked up a plethora of awards for its beers since then, as attested to by the wall of certificates behind their cellar door bar. Some of their beers are ranged nationally through major retail chains, too.

Yet, in something of a reminder of how far craft beer has to go before it can claim to be truly accepted, their impact in their home town of Port Macquarie has been negligible. In fact, their Wicked Elf Pale Ale is pretty much their only beer you will find on tap there, adorning a single spot at the Town Green. Maybe when it's pouring on two taps in the town we can say the revolution truly has succeeded ...

Brewer's food match
Full-flavoured game, duck and spicy foods

Availability
Year round

Where to find it
Good independent bottle shops, BWS, Dan Murphy's

Brewery and cellar door location
Unit 1/58 Uralla Road, Port Macquarie, New South Wales

Brewery website
www.thelittlebrewingcompany.com.au

Pale Ale

LITTLE CREATURES BREWING

 **American pale ale** **5.2%**  **4.8-5°C** **Pint glass**

TASTING NOTES If you're reading this book, chances are you're au fait with this beer. For the few that aren't, it possesses fruity hops, sweetness and quenching bitterness in such perfect harmony that it helped change an entire nation's drinking culture.

THE STORY What's left to say about this beer? Since it was first released as Little Creatures Live when the brewery's HQ on the Fremantle waterfront was opened in 2000, it has done more than any other to change Australia's drinking habits. Inspired by the aromatic pale ales of the US, such as Sierra Nevada's classic, it was the first local brew to use whole hop flowers from the Pacific Northwest to achieve its goal. Many regard its 2002 crowning as Champion Beer at the Australian International Beer Awards as a watershed moment.

Beautifully balanced and always enticing, it remains a go-to beer for countless drinkers across the land and, following the opening of a new Little Creatures Brewery in Geelong, with the business financially boosted by a 2012 takeover by Lion, it is set to win over even more.

Availability
Year round

Where to find it
Available at all good bottle shops Australia-wide

Brewery and cellar door locations
40 Mews Road, Fremantle, Western Australia; Cnr Fyans and Swanston streets, Geelong, Victoria

Brewery website
www.littlecreatures.com.au

Alpha Pale Ale
MATILDA BAY BREWING COMPANY

 American pale ale 5.2%  4-8°C Shaker glass, US pint

TASTING NOTES This serial trophy-winner is as bang-to-rights an American pale ale you'll find in Australia. Lifted hop aromatics range from sherbet to citrus to lemon, while it's just as zesty in the mouth. Clean yet full-flavoured, bitter yet balanced. Delicious.

THE STORY In 2013, Matilda Bay launched a billboard campaign based around the brewery's family of beers. Tucked away right at the back, like the black sheep or funny uncle, was Alpha Pale Ale. Its position might lead you to assume it's the least of their beers, one for which there is no great affection. Yet, also in 2013, Alpha Pale Ale was named the Champion Beer of Australia at the prestigious Australian International Beer Awards – the highest accolade any beer in Australia can receive. It is also available more widely than most beers that pack this much flavour with this much panache, thanks to Matilda Bay being part of the global SABMiller business.

So why is it tucked at the back of the family photo? Simple economics. Fat Yak, Matilda Bay's pale (forgive the pun) imitation of the same style shifts astronomical numbers by comparison. Still, if you're keen to discover how top-notch American pale ales taste fresh without crossing the Pacific, grab a four-pack of Alpha; who knows, if more of us do, it may one day warrant a more prominent position in future family photos.

Brewer's food match
Maple-glazed pork ribs

Availability
Year round

Where to find it
Dan Murphy's, selected bottle shops

Brewery and cellar door location
89 Bertie Street, Port Melbourne, Victoria

Brewery website
www.matildabay.com.au

Ticket Booth Pale Ale
SIDESHOW BREWERS

 American pale ale **4.7%** **5-8°C**  **Dimpled mug or American pint glass**

TASTING NOTES Heavy, late hopping lends this cloudy amber beer floral, citrus and lemon sherbet aromas, backed up by plenty of caramel. Distinct West Coast US hop flavours sit alongside rich caramel and toffee malts too, before a restrained bitterness brings the curtain down.

THE STORY This is a beer that came from out of nowhere and, pretty much overnight, started shifting six-packs faster than anything else at some of Melbourne's specialist bottle shops. In part, its success was down to the fact that it was the first release from a guy who lived locally: Clyde D'Angelis took one of his home brew recipes along to a mate's brewery, Kooinda in Heidelberg, to create it on a commercial scale.

But local pride and word of mouth can only take so much of the credit. Future batches of the Ticket Booth Pale Ale have also shifted units fast, down to the fact that it's a beer that nails the style. The relationship with Kooinda has continued too, both in the form of further Sideshow Brewers' releases and a festive collaboration for Christmas 2013 called Decembeer.

Brewer's food match
Grilled pork sausages, provolone cheese, olives, hot salami, prosciutto, spicy pizza, veal schnitzel

Availability
Year round

Where to find it
At all good craft beer outlets

Brewery location
28 Culverlands Street, Heidelberg West, Victoria

Brewery website
www.sideshowbrewers.com.au

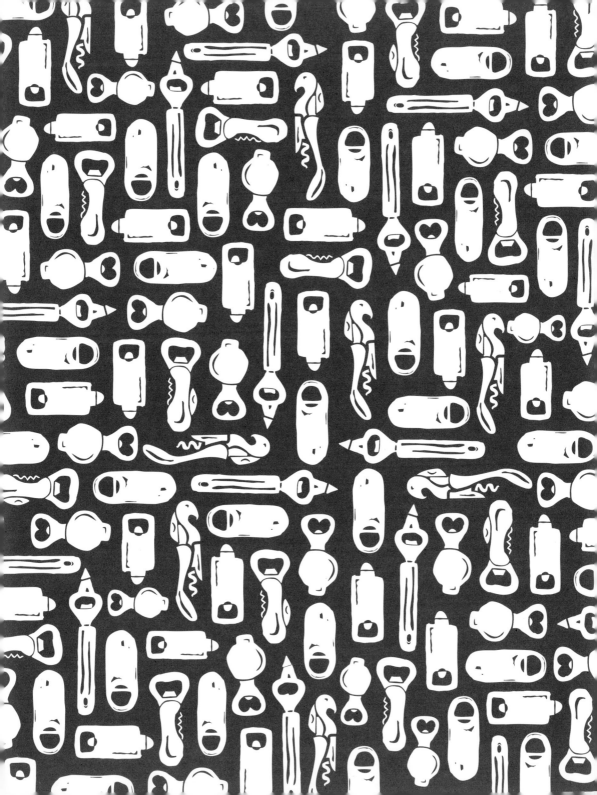

IPAs

Has any beer captured the imagination of the new wave of brewers - and indeed drinkers - around the world in the same way as India pale ale ('IPA' for short)?

This style, which these days tends to act as a showcase for hops, is another with a long tradition that has been grabbed with both hands by American craft brewers and turned into a seriously amped-up version of the original.

So what was the original India pale ale? The most commonly told tale about this wonderful beer style is that the brewers supplying the British colony on the Indian subcontinent realised that their ales had a better chance of arriving in reasonable condition if they were highly hopped and higher in alcohol, as both hops and alcohol act as a preservative.

There is a second, less commonly told, tale that accompanies this. The location sometimes changes, but essentially the story is that ships destined for India carrying this hoppy, boozy cargo were shipwrecked not far off the British coastline. This allowed locals to sample such beers for the first time, declare them wonderful and kickstart a market for them in the UK.

Such tales have been picked apart by fastidious historians of beer, but there are elements of truth hidden within. What is known for certain is that English ales were sent to the Indian subcontinent and, after weeks at sea in wooden barrels, could arrive in rather poor condition. It is also known that brewers were advised to add extra hops to beers when sending them overseas from England – but this knowledge predates India pale ales and was used by brewers supplying countries other than India, too.

Either way, by the 1830s, the phrase 'East India pale ale' was being used to describe these hoppy, relatively high-alcohol beers; indeed, according to historian Martyn Cornell, the first recorded use of the phrase 'India pale ale' was actually in Australia, in the *Sydney Gazette and New South Wales Advertiser* of 29 August 1829.

A century and a half later, this style became the perfect conduit for many of the American craft beer revolution's brewers that were following the mantra 'bigger is better'. Using the wonderfully pungent, citrusy and piny hop varieties developed in the Pacific Northwest, they took IPA to another plane. Since then, the sky has been the limit when it comes to experimentation and taking hopping (and indeed alcohol) levels to extremes with the IPA style.

There have been double IPAs, imperial IPAs, black IPAs (something of an oxymoron, given it means creating a black pale ale), white IPAs (usually featuring Belgian yeasts) and much more besides.

The love of such beers has been taken up by Australian brewers and drinkers alike. Indeed, in a nationwide poll of drinkers run by beer venue The Local Taphouse to find the most popular Australian craft beers in 2013, more than a quarter of the top 100 were IPAs.

With such beers, which are always best fresh, drinkers should be expecting big hop aromatics and similarly hop-dominated flavours, all balanced with enough malt sweetness to stop the bitterness from getting out of control. Most brewed in Australia are inspired by the American approach, although you will occasionally find a locally brewed English IPA, with James Squire's recently reworked and readily available Stow Away (which almost made the pages of this book) a good introduction to the latter.

TOP OF THE HOPS

My top three 'straight' IPAs:
FERAL HOP HOG
RIVERSIDE BREWING 77 IPA
LITTLE CREATURES BREWING IPA

My top three 'other' IPAs:
MURRAY'S CRAFT BREWING ICON 2IPA
KOOINDA BREWERY BLACK IPA
BRIDGE ROAD BREWERS BLING BLING IMPERIAL IPA

Cunning Ninja Imperial IPA
BACCHUS BREWING

 Imperial American IPA  12.0% 8°C Snifter (brandy glass)

TASTING NOTES One of many huge beers from Bacchus, this imperial IPA is chock-full of hops but their fruity, spicy nature plays second fiddle to the intense burnt toffee and licorice aromas that come from the mountain of malt needed to hold them check. Surprisingly smooth for a beer of this insane hoppiness and alcohol content, with complex spicy, herbal and stewed-fruit flavours alongside the bitterness.

THE STORY There is little, perhaps nothing, normal about Queensland's Bacchus Brewing. Based in a large warehouse that's also home to a successful home-brewing business, the brewery is made up of a series of small brewhouses, each capable of knocking out 50 litres at a time, plus one larger system. Sometimes they will all be used to create the same beer at the same time; other times, Bacchus might brew half a dozen different beers on the same day.

Not only are their methods unusual, the scope and sheer oddness of some of their releases is pretty out there too. Sure, you can pick up a straight pale ale if you want. Alternatively, you can grab a raspberry and white chocolate pilsner, a puckering fruity sour or an incredibly high-alcohol, barrel-aged specialty. The Cunning Ninja comes from the ultra-high ABV part of the Bacchus range and is one of the most cultishly admired beers from this most cultish of breweries.

Brewer's food match
Cheese

Availability
Year round

Where to find it
At the Bacchus Brewing brewery

Brewery and cellar door location
2 Christine Place, Capalaba, Queensland

Brewery website
www.bacchusbrewing.com.au

Hell Hound India Black Ale

BLACK DOG BREWERY

 India black ale 7.0%  6°C IPA or tulip glass

TASTING NOTES Black Dog's take on the faddish black IPA style is a heavy-hitting beer nerd's delight. Pouring a thick, voluminous nigh-on-black with a mocha head like a dense porter, it hits you first with pine and chocolate orange aromas, then follows up with tons of hop flavour and bitterness balanced by dark cocoa and rounded roast malt.

THE STORY Black Dog has one of the most unique stories of any brewery in Australia. James Booth is the fourth-generation winemaker at Taminick Cellars, which operates from a beautiful, rustic old brick building lined with creaking barriques a few unsealed kilometres down the road from Glenrowan.

He decided to add beer to the family's offerings, launching Black Dog on a home-built 70-litre system, before upgrading late in 2013 to an impressive Italian setup. He has held beer versus wine dinners at which every beverage on the table was crafted by his hand and, after launching with a range of more approachable beers, has become more experimental over time, with this India black ale a fine take on a relatively new style that pulls no punches.

Brewer's food match
Smoky barbecue ribs

Availability
Seasonal

Where to find it
Selected retailers

Brewery and cellar door location
339 Booth Road, Taminick, Victoria
(located at Taminick Cellars winery)

Brewery website
www.blackdogbrewery.com.au

Speakeasy IPA

BOOTLEG BREWERY

 American IPA 5.5%  3°C IPA glass

TASTING NOTES This rusty, almost amber-coloured IPA wastes no time capturing your attention with its muscular peach and pine aromas. It's based on West Coast IPAs from the US, so it packs in heaps of hops, with just about enough biscuit and caramel malt sweetness to keep the roaring bitterness in check.

THE STORY In fifteen years as head brewer at Margaret River's Bootleg Brewery, Michael Brookes has turned his hand to many a beer. There has been the safety-first core range made up of wheat beers, gently hopped ales and lagers, and then the more adventurous stuff: high-ABV barley wines, barrel-ageing, and beers featuring locally sourced fruit. Yet if he were to choose a style that he

could quaff the rest of his days – quite probably in between blasts on his mountain bike and surfboard – it would be the kind of IPA made famous by the brewers of the west coast of the US. Quite how he never got around to brewing such a beer of his own until 2013 is a mystery.

Still, having experimented with heavy hopping regimes with Bootleg's popular annual release, the Black Market Black IPA, the Speakeasy finally arrived, increasing the brewery's annual hop bill but quite possibly reducing his personal air miles across the Pacific, now that he can drink fresh West Coast IPA at home.

Brewer's food match
Barbecue duck tacos

Availability
Year round

Where to find it
Good independent liquor stores in Perth, southwest Western Australia

Brewery and cellar door location
Puzey Road, Wilyabrup, Western Australia

Brewery website
www.bootlegbrewery.com.au

Bling Bling Imperial IPA
BRIDGE ROAD BREWERS

 Imperial IPA 8.5% 7.5°C IPA glass

TASTING NOTES This is a fantastic local example of the huge IPAs popularised in America. Fantastic because, while it is stuffed to the gills with hops, producing predominantly citrus and tropical characteristics, there's enough of a smooth caramel backbone to balance the high bittering.

THE STORY Of all the brewers in the country, Bridge Road founder Ben Kraus probably has the closest relationship with Aussie hops. His brewery is based just down the road from one of Hop Product Australia's main farms; he has produced multiple single-hop IPAs using Australian hop varieties; and every year he creates a harvest ale that features a new, unreleased (sometimes never-to-be-released) experimental variety from the nearby farm, picked fresh that day

and added, still wet, to the brew. One year he chose a variety that was set to be struck off HPA's breeding program, but the beer turned out so well that the hop was saved and is now sold worldwide as Vic Secret. Hoppiest of all his beers, however, is the Bling Bling, first brewed in 2013. A souped-up version of his Bling IPA, drunk fresh it's a powerful yet balanced local interpretation of the beers that tend to send Aussie beer lovers into raptures whenever they head stateside.

Brewer's food match
Slightly spicy or oily dishes

Availability
Year round

Where to find it
Specialty craft beer outlets

Brewery and cellar door location
50 Ford Street, Beechworth, Victoria

Brewery website
www.bridgeroadbrewers.com.au

Berserker Amber IPA

EKIM BREWING CO

 Amber IPA 7.2% 12-14°C Tulip glass

TASTING NOTES This hazy amber IPA sees piny hops mingling with creamy toffee malt aromas. There's a creamy mouthfeel too, in which mountains of smooth caramel play off palate-tickling hops, with enough sweetness to keep the high level of IBUs in check.

THE STORY Sydney brewer Mike Jorgensen loves hops, in particular pungently aromatic American hops. Almost all of his beers use them in varying – usually rather high – amounts. As such, he is one of the most vocal local brewers when it comes to insisting that his beers are drunk as fresh as possible, before the effects of age can wither them. His eye-catching, cartoonish labels request that the contents are consumed within three months – a tight timescale by anyone's reckoning. It's an approach that is doing him little harm; having started out brewing on fellow brewery Happy Goblin's tiny set-up, in 2013 he began embarking upon significant expansion.

Given the hoppy beers in his range go from a pale ale to India pale ale to a black IPA to a hoppy porter (spotted a theme yet?), it seems sensible to highlight one of the most recent releases, the Berserker: a hefty meeting of rich, chewy caramel malts and piny American hops that sits somewhere in the middle of the Ekim spectrum.

Brewer's food match
Curry, burgers, spicy Asian fare, fish, chicken, tangy or mild blue cheese

Availability
Year round in small/limited batches

Where to find it
On tap in Sydney, Brisbane and Melbourne

Brewery location
Mount Kuringai, New South Wales

Brewery website
www.ekimbrewing.com.au

Hop Hog IPA
FERAL BREWING

 India pale ale   5.8%   7°C   Spiegelau IPA glass

TASTING NOTES The dictionary definition for American IPA? Dense clouds of citrus and pine aromas reach your nose well before the glass gets anywhere near your mouth; upon drinking, those same hop characteristics are balanced perfectly by a sweet malt backbone before a wave of drying bitterness sweeps across the palate in readiness to go again.

THE STORY Less a beer than a modern Australian icon. Feral's flagship is such a consistently wonderful beer that, when it fails to pick up a trophy at a beer awards, mere eyebrow-raising isn't enough – only the flabbergasted dropping of jaws will suffice.

For years it was the subject of awed rumours outside the champion brewery's home state. Head brewer Brendan Varis is perhaps Australia's greatest exponent of the 'fresh is best' mantra when it comes to hoppy beers – he has one beer on his roster, the Imperial IPA Tusk, that is only sent to venues that promise to tap it the very day it arrives. As such, he refused to send Hop Hog across the Nullarbor until he could guarantee refrigerated delivery. Once that was secured, the first kegs that landed at the Great Northern Hotel in North Carlton (run by the brewery's co-founder) lured beer pilgrims to its bar like crusaders chasing an aromatic Holy Grail. Four years on, the beer is well on its way to conquering the entire country. Essentially, anyone wanting to know just what an excellent American-style IPA tastes like has two options. One: save up a few thousand dollars and fly to the west coast of the US. Two: save up a few dollars and buy a Hop Hog.

Brewer's food match
A fiery Madras curry

Availability
Year round

Where to find it
On tap and at good bottle shops
Australia-wide

Brewery and cellar door location
152 Haddrill Road, Baskerville,
Western Australia

Brewery website
www.feralbrewing.com.au

Australian IPA

HAWTHORN BREWING COMPANY

 Australian IPA 5.8% 4-6°C Pint/tumbler

TASTING NOTES The first Hawthorn beer to push the boat out a little further is also one that showcases contemporary Australian hops as well as any other. It's so awash with tropical fruits, both on the nose and palate, that it's reminiscent of Wrigley's Juicy Fruit chewing gum. Soft on the palate, with the hops balanced perfectly by the malt, it's a dangerously drinkable drop.

THE STORY Whether the Hawthorn Brewing Company ever ends up calling Hawthorn home remains to be seen. For now, they continue to enjoy commercial success having their beers brewed by BrewPack in New South Wales and, with contract brewing becoming a more prevalent and accepted means of bringing flavoursome beer to market, it may

be that the self-proclaimed 'Flavour Merchants' never drop anchor with a brewery or bar in their home suburb.

Having established themselves with a range of well made, if unadventurous, beers in 2013, they did something a little different with this recipe for a highly hopped Australian IPA. It was sent to the International Beer Challenge in the UK, where it picked up a major trophy for Best Ale Over 5 Per Cent. Suitably emboldened, the group of mates behind the company began working on a series of limited releases that should allow their more creative urges to come to the fore.

Brewer's food match
Spicy food, curries

Availability
Year round

Where to find it
At selected shops Australia-wide

Brewery location
Smeaton Grange, New South Wales

Brewery website
www.hawthornbrewing.com.au

Road Trip IPA
HOLGATE BREWHOUSE

 American IPA   6.0%  4-6°C   Jar or tulip glass

TASTING NOTES This beer uses all American hops, from the earliest possible moment in the brew right through to the end, to create an IPA with hop characteristics that tick boxes marked pine, passionfruit, grapefruit and marmalade – not to mention solid bitterness, too.

THE STORY Time spent in the UK and the US at points in the 90s initially inspired Paul Holgate to open a microbrewery, originally brewing from the back of his house and now (in a seemingly constant state of expansion) at the former Keating's Hotel in Woodend. And it was a holiday with his family in the American Pacific Northwest many years later – a region that is home to many of the hop varieties that helped fuel the American craft beer revolution – that sparked the Road Trip. Having an American as part of the brewing team probably didn't hurt either. Taking inspiration from the highly hopped, highly aromatic IPAs of that region, and featuring hop additions at pretty much every single step imaginable in the brewing process, it rapidly became one of their most popular releases. And, as with many beers in their range, it is one that is being constantly refined for the better, too.

Brewer's food match
American-style burger, fried chicken or spicy curry

Availability
Year round

Where to find it
Many good bottle shops and restaurants Australia-wide; check website for full list of stockists

Brewery and cellar door location
79 High Street, Woodend, Victoria

Brewery website
www.holgatebrewhouse.com

Horns Up Rye IPA

HOPDOG BEERWORKS

 American IPA 5.8%  4°C Pint or goblet

TASTING NOTES This surprisingly light-coloured, pale golden IPA throws off huge hop aromatics from its towering, white fluffy head: grapefruit, grape, kiwifruit and pine batter the senses. There's a touch of spice and something herbal in the taste too, with just enough malt to hold it together, and a bold yet controlled bitterness.

THE STORY HopDog BeerWorks could not have existed just a few years ago. The twisted brainchild of heavy-metal enthusiast Tim Thomas, it operates on a tiny brewery set-up in a factory unit in Nowra, two hours south of Sydney. He brews beers with names such as 'Children of Darkness' and 'American Werewolf in Belgium', isn't afraid to throw all manner of fruits, spices, homemade biscuits and weird yeasts into beers and then seal them in barrels for months on end, and many of his beers appear once and once only. As the name suggests, he's something of a hop fiend, although his Belgian-style beers are often superior to his hop bombs. That said, his flagship Horns Up Rye IPA is probably the best introduction to HopDog, both because it is brewed regularly and also because its head-on collision of big, chewy, spicy malts with a ton of hop bitterness sums up his rather no-holds-barred, seat-of-the-pants approach to brewing.

Brewer's food match
Great with curries, chilli, Thai and Cajun

Availability
Year round

Where to find it
See website for full list of stockists

Brewery and cellar door location
2/175 Princes Highway, South Nowra, New South Wales

Brewery website
www.hopdog.com.au

Apocalypso IPA
ILLAWARRA BREWING COMPANY

 **American IPA**   **6.0%**   **6-10°C**   **Pint glass**

TASTING NOTES If the apocalypse tastes like this, sign me up for a ticket to the end of the world. Originally intended as a one-off release, this grapefruit, passionfruit and citrus delight proved so popular it's now part of Illawarra's year-round brewing schedule. Wonderfully aromatic, with heaps of fruity hop and caramel malt flavours and well-integrated bitterness, this great-looking beer is one of a growing number of fine IPAs coming out of young New South Wales breweries.

THE STORY Former Illawarra head brewer Andrew Gow has been making waves at Mornington Peninsula Brewery since late 2010. Before leaving Illawarra, he was charged with finding brewers to take up the reins. Rather than seek applications from outside, he offered to train up two of the young staff working around the brewery and its bar, Ashur Hall and Shaun Blissett. As the pair are only too happy to admit, within just a few weeks they'd gone from cleaning toilets to making beer on a commercial scale.

Clearly their mentor had spotted fine potential as, within a few months, one of their first beers, a Kolsch, took out a trophy at the country's biggest beer awards. They've gone on to help transform the brewery – formerly known as predominantly a contract facility for other breweries – into one respected for its own beers, which are found increasingly broadly in the better bars of New South Wales.

Brewer's food match
Steak, lamb chops, pork or beef ribs, general meat products

Availability
Year round

Where to find it
Selected venues throughout Sydney, Newcastle and Victoria

Brewery location
Unit 4/83–85 Montague Street, North Wollongong, New South Wales

Brewery website
www.illawarrabrewingco.com.au

Double IPA

KAIJU! BEER (FORMERLY MONSTER MASH)

 American imperial IPA 9.1% 6-8°C  *Spiegelau IPA glass*

TASTING NOTES As beautiful as it is big, this beer pours an appealing rusty copper colour with a lasting fluffy head. Resinous, piny and citrus hops mix with some sweet booze on the nose in a beer that is well balanced and clean despite the clearly huge hopping regime.

THE STORY The arrival of Melbourne's Moon Dog in 2011 signalled something of a sea change for Australian breweries. Determined to tear up the rules of the game, they launched into a series of wild, outlandish beers with equally colourful (and frequently obtuse) names and labels.

Two years later, it meant that the decision of the brothers behind Kaiju! (formerly named Monster Mash, but renamed following a challenge by the manufacturers of Monster energy drink) to enter the market with a 9.1 per cent double IPA raised fewer eyebrows than it might once have done. Callum and Nat Reeves already had a cider, Golden Axe, that was making great inroads in the Victorian market; this double IPA, complete with superb, eye-catching artwork on its label by young Ohio artist Mikey Burton, soon ensured beer drinkers were aware of them, too.

Brewer's food match
Rare dry-aged rib-eye steak

Availability
Year round (limited)

Where to find it
Slowbeer, Small Patch, The Park Hotel Werribee, Caulfield Cellars, McCoppins

Brewery location
Derrimut (Cavalier), Victoria

Brewery website
www.kaijubeer.com.au

Black IPA (formerly Full Nelson)

KOOINDA BREWERY

 Black IPA   7.0%   6-8°C   IPA glass

TASTING NOTES This is what happens when two tribes go to war. As fierce a black IPA as has been released in Australia, this beer is one in which the rampaging horde of Kiwi hops comes up against an equally powerful foe in the form of slightly roasted malts, with the war ending in a bloody but marvellous draw.

THE STORY In 2012, it seemed that every collaboration between an Aussie and an international brewer – and pretty much every other limited release from a local brewer – was a Black IPA. Essentially conceived as a bit of fun (the 'P' in IPA stands for 'pale', so the challenge was to create beers that were black in colour yet possessed little to none of the roastier characteristics normally associated with black beers), the craze, which has since died down a little, threw up some fantastic beers.

Among them were Temple's Midnight, several from Mountain Goat and Bridge Road, and this from Kooinda. It was initially called the Full Nelson due to its use of heaps of the Kiwi hop Nelson Sauvin, a notoriously aggressive hop. The brewers at Kooinda used it aggressively in the beer too, and yet somehow managed to keep its rampant aggression in check to create a beer that is undoubtedly fierce yet balanced and much loved throughout the country.

Availability
Year round

Brewery website
www.kooinda.com

Brewery and cellar door location
28 Culverlands Street, Heidelberg West, Victoria

IPA

LITTLE CREATURES BREWING

 Australian IPA   6.4%   4.8-5°C   IPA glass

TASTING NOTES This is a carnival for the senses, overflowing with wonderful hop aromas – floral, tropical, spicy and citrusy – and a depth of the flavours to match, all balanced in inimitable Little Creatures style; so well balanced, in fact, you can scarcely believe it registers 60 IBUs (International Bitterness Units).

THE STORY Little Creatures' core range rarely changes. But, in 2013, seven years after the last permanent addition to the line-up, the brewers were granted a long-awaited wish: to brew an IPA. And boy, did they do a good job. Quite possibly the most dangerously drinkable beer in Australia (6.4 per cent of smooth, fruity goodness), it bears the hallmarks of their pale ale at its best... then ramps them up to eleven.

What that translates to is a cloud of enticing, fruity aromas atop a beer so carefully designed that, despite the relatively high IBU level, the bitterness is barely perceptible. Given the brewery's reach, especially following its takeover by Lion, it means that pretty much every single bottle store in Australia now has access to an excellent, hoppy-as-hell IPA. That means that this beer is likely to blaze a palate-enlightening trail across the country, just like its predecessor did before.

Availability
Year round

Where to find it
Available at all good bottle shops Australia-wide

Brewery and cellar door locations
40 Mews Road, Fremantle, Western Australia; Cnr Fyans and Swanston streets, Geelong, Victoria

Brewery website
www.littlecreatures.com.au

India Pale Ale / Double-Hopped IPA

LOBETHAL BIERHAUS

 British-style IPA with an American twist   5.9%   Chilled   Largest glass possible

TASTING NOTES Two beers in one here, with Lobethal's original India Pale Ale an earthy, copper-coloured English-style IPA. The superb double-hopped version shows just how much late hopping can change a beer, adding lashings of wonderful grapefruit and citrus aromas and flavours, while leaving the beer refreshingly lean and dry.

THE STORY Warned as a youngster by his father not to enter the pub business and thus risk becoming a 'drunk's labourer', Alistair Turnbull nevertheless followed his life's dream and became a brewer after a couple of decades working for banks.

It has proved a wise move, with Lobethal Bierhaus becoming the most highly regarded South Australian microbrewery, with Al's beers always on tap at Adelaide's iconic bar, The Wheaty, and Lobethal regularly collaborating with out-there Kiwi superstar brewers the Yeastie Boys. In the case of the latter, the beers have always been named after the respective brewers' dogs, with the annual collaborations proving so successful they've had to buy more pets. Of Lobethal's core range, the Double-Hopped IPA is the highlight, one that will hopefully be seen more regularly and more widely following 2013's brewery expansion.

Brewer's food match
Spicy dishes, such as curry

Availability
Year round

Where to find it
Throughout South Australia in independent bottle shops, restaurants and hotels

Brewery and cellar door location
3A Main Street, Lobethal, South Australia

Brewery website
www.bierhaus.com.au

IPA

MORNINGTON PENINSULA BREWERY

 India pale ale 6.4% 4-6°C Spiegelau IPA glass

TASTING NOTES In its very early days, this IPA was one that would let its bitterness off the leash a little too freely. Now, despite having lost none of its punch, its peach and pine hops still launch a full-frontal assault, but do so with more composure, resulting in one of Australia's finest IPAs.

THE STORY With three of them (the brown ale, porter and Russian imperial stout) making the pages of this book, it's clear Mornington Peninsula brewer Andrew Gow knows a thing or two about creating top-notch dark beers. He also enjoys playing with hops, particularly new varieties.

Ever a student of new beer styles or ingredients from overseas, he has been among the first Australians to release beers featuring hop varieties such as the idiosyncratic Sorachi Ace and Mosaic. The former still appears with regularity in the brewery's Kolsch, while the latter was used to create a quite delightful fruit-bomb of a single-hop IPA in 2013. This IPA, part of the brewery's year-round roster, and inspired by those from the US, is one of the boldest available in Australia. Look out for a seasonally released imperial IPA, too.

Brewer's food match
Strong cheese, hot and spicy foods, curries

Availability
Year round

Where to find it
Good bottle shops and bars in Queensland and Victoria

Brewery and cellar door location
72 Watt Road, Mornington, Victoria

Brewery website
www.mpbrew.com.au

IPA

MOUNTAIN GOAT

 India pale ale   **6.2%**   **3°C**   **Tulip glass**

TASTING NOTES A fine IPA that, in draught form at least, has become hoppier and leaner over time. A blend of New World hops creates lovely citrus and pine aromas that sit hand-in-hand with caramel malts before going out with a bang of firm, lingering hop bitterness.

THE STORY Mountain Goat's IPA has been through many iterations. A few years ago, their original IPA was an organic beer that bit the dust when the brewery underwent significant rebranding. A new IPA appeared as the first-ever Rare Breed release following the rebranding. It was a US-inspired, highly hopped take on the style, albeit with plenty of chewy malts in there too, and took little time establishing itself as a firm fan favourite. Since then,

Mountain Goat has brewed various black IPAs, a coffee IPA, a double IPA, imperial IPAs, a rye IPA and a red IPA.

The original Rare Breed IPA has itself been refined into an even hoppier, leaner version and has proved so popular that the Rare Breed prefix was dropped and it became the third member of their year-round line-up. As such, the bottled product is now produced offsite by Asahi Premium Beverages to ensure they can meet demand. Keep an eye out for the olive-green goat tap head that signifies it's pouring at venues, as all draught product is still produced by the home team at their iconic warehouse in Richmond.

Brewer's food match
Smoked or barbecued meats; slow-cooked goat is perfect

Availability
Year round

Where to find it
At bottle shops Australia-wide

Brewery and cellar door location
80 North Street, Richmond, Victoria

Brewery website
www.goatbeer.com.au

Icon 2IPA

MURRAY'S CRAFT BREWING

 India pale ale   7.5%   4-10°C   **US-style shaker pint or new US IPA glass**

TASTING NOTES An Icon by name... it's a crystalline copper ale that achieves a perfect blend of citrus and passionfruit aromas – with a touch of spice, too – that leap from the glass with balancing, biscuity malts. One of the very first, and still finest, big IPAs in the country.

THE STORY If I had to pick an epiphany beer, the one that really flicked the light switch on the Australian beer world, this is it. A few months after moving to Melbourne, a friend from the beer industry insisted I hand over my last few dollars for a stubby of Icon. Rising to meet me from the glass was the most overwhelming, wantonly seductive aroma I had encountered in any Australian beer to that point. It was reminiscent of my first encounter with Dogfish Head's 90 Minute IPA on a previous trip to the US.

Since then, the all-pervading influence of the American craft-beer industry has seen palate-assaulting IPAs and double/imperial IPAs become more commonplace. As a result, the once-a-year-released Icon appears to have become something of a forgotten hero. But whether you have tried it before and forgotten, or are yet to experience it, it's worth discovering again and again.

Brewer's food match
Thai jungle curry; strong, hard vintage cheddar

Availability
Draught year round; bottle seasonal

Where to find it
Available from website and Australia-wide at good craft beer venues

Brewery and cellar door location
3443 Nelson Bay Road, Bobs Farm, New South Wales

Brewery website
www.murraysbrewingco.com.au

India Pale Ale (Gluten Free)

O'BRIEN BEER

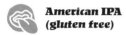 **American IPA (gluten free)**   **6.0%**   **8°C**   **Nonic or tulip glass**

TASTING NOTES This pours a brilliant, clear gold, albeit with little in the way of a head, and exhibits plentiful pineapple, grapefruit and pine aromas over a clean base beer that uses millet and sorghum. Will change the opinion of many on gluten-free beers.

THE STORY The 2013 Australian International Beer Awards saw the first time a gold medal was awarded to a gluten-free beer. It was the culmination of a long journey for John O'Brien, who first started out on the path to create a decent-tasting gluten-free beer back in 1998 when he was diagnosed with coeliac disease. It took until 2005 for the first O'Brien beer to be released, and a further eight before his Belgian ale topped the podium, but, along with brewing colleague and fellow coeliac sufferer Andrew Lavery,

he is now responsible for a series of impressive gluten-free beers. This India pale ale is brewed with sorghum and millet instead of barley and possesses all of the enticing citrus, pineapple and pine aromas one would expect in a New World IPA. You can now visit them at their Rebellion Brewery bar in Ballarat and see how they go about their business, too.

Brewer's food match
Thai green curried prawns

Availability
Seasonal (spring, September–March)

Where to find it
Selected bottle shops

Brewery and cellar door location
47 Mair Street East, Ballarat, Victoria

Brewery website
www.rebellionbrewing.com.au

77 IPA

RIVERSIDE BREWING COMPANY

 American IPA   7.7%   4-6°C   IPA or tulip glass

TASTING NOTES Acknowledged as one of the finest IPAs in Australia, the 77 hits you with massive grapefruit and pine aromas from the off, with the hops leaving you in no doubt as to who is boss on the palate, either. Bold, resinous marmalade and pine flavours dominate, leading to a solid yet contained bitterness in a beer that's lean for its size, too.

THE STORY The closest thing to a river anywhere near Riverside Brewing is a storm drain across the road. But, given the incredible way in which Dave Padden's switch from home brewer to the commercial realm has taken the Australian craft beer scene by storm, it's easy to forget that spot of largesse. After a couple of years spent touring existing breweries – often buying up their old gear – Riverside launched into the market with a range of US-inspired, predominantly hop-forward beers, and impressed from the outset. Already established as one of the New South Wales' nascent scene's star breweries, this marvellous IPA is as good as any you'll lay your hands on.

Brewer's food match
Curry

Availability
Year round

Where to find it
Currently Sydney and Newcastle only; Melbourne and Brisbane soon

Brewery and cellar door location
2 North Rocks Road, North Parramatta, New South Wales

Brewery website
www.riversidebrewing.com.au

IPA

SMILING SAMOYED

 **India pale ale** **6.8%** **5-6°C** **Tulip glass**

TASTING NOTES This IPA looks to America for its inspiration and hits the nail on the head with prominent pine and citrus aromas. In the mouth, it perhaps rushes a little towards its resinous, bitter finish without pausing for those fruity flavours to come into play, but it's a fine, clean, striking beer from a promising brewery.

THE STORY Husband-and-wife team Simon Dunstone and Kate Henning had comfortable, well-paid jobs in Adelaide – the former a software developer, the latter a litigation lawyer. But, realising their souls needed sustenance more than their bank accounts, they jacked in their careers, upped sticks and headed to Myponga to take over a brewery in the 500-soul town. They steadily overhauled the charmingly rustic venue, installed a shiny new brewery (with family support), and introduced locals and tourists to a fine range of beers while also stocking their fridges with plenty of favourites from other brewers.

The 12 Paws Pale Ale, named, like the brewery, after their three Samoyed dogs, is the biggest seller, but this resinous-yet-refined IPA is possibly better still, registering 6.8 per cent ABV and giving more bite than their ever-present, smiling pets.

Brewer's food match
FruChocs

Availability
Year round

Where to find it
Good craft beer outlets in South Australia

Brewery and cellar door location
48 Main South Road, Myponga, South Australia

Brewery website
www.smilingsamoyed.com.au

BRITISH
AND IRISH
ALES

British and Irish Ales

Gathering together this clutch of beers under the heading 'British and Irish ales' makes for a pretty broad church. What's more, as you'll read in the introductions to many of the other chapters in this book, there are plenty of other beers in these pages that can trace their lineage back to the British Isles.

But, as is also made clear in those chapters, in the past few decades many such styles, some of which had been practically lost and were rarely brewed, have been revived, reinvigorated and reinvented as something shiny and new. This collection features beers created by Australian brewers that aim to stay true to the more traditional ales brewed in the UK and Ireland.

Such beers are in the minority when compared to those that take their lead from the US, but they still make for a pretty eclectic collection. Furthermore, even when setting out to create a beer that is, for all intents and purposes, an interpretation of an Old World beer, many brewers cannot resist the temptation to add a New World flourish, decorating them with tropical hops.

Thus here you will find low-alcohol English bitters featuring Australian and New Zealand hops alongside more authentic re-creations: pale ales or darker, richer malt-led ales that feature more subdued, earthy or gently floral hop varieties that originate in the UK.

Alongside such beers are a number of higher-alcohol ales. In most cases, these are based on English strong or old ales: typically sweet and malty, with distinct fruity esters and complex, warming, multi-layered flavours. There is also one strong Scotch ale, the Seeing Double, that adds smoky peated distilling malt to the mix.

One might question the inclusion of Coopers Sparkling Ale here, given it is often recognised as the originator of the Australian pale ale style. However, it is a re-creation of fruity English ales and shares more in common with these beers than those found in the pale ales chapter.

With so many different styles gathered in one place it is impossible to draw much in the way of commonality between them. What can be said is that English hops, of which East Kent Goldings and Fuggles are the two most frequently used in Australia, share similarities with the noble hops of Europe, in that they have a subtlety and elegance, generally lending a softer, broader bitterness on the palate. Hop usage in these beers also tends to be at a far lower level than those favoured by many brewers of New World beer styles, who will add them in greater volumes and at many more stages in the brewing process than in traditional British and Irish beers.

Another common characteristic can be the fullness imparted on beers by British malts – a fullness both in terms of flavour and mouthfeel. Yeast strains from the old country, particularly those typically used in English ales, often impart fruity characteristics upon the beer during fermentation, distinct from the generally cleaner impact of American ale yeasts.

TOP OF THE HOPS

4 PINES BREWING COMPANY ESB
HARGREAVES HILL ESB
MURRAY'S CRAFT BREWING PUNCH & JUDY

ESB

4 PINES BREWING COMPANY

 Bitter   **5.4%**   **6-8°C** **Pint**

TASTING NOTES It's everything one should expect from a strong English bitter: earthy hops and rich toffee and raisin aromas lead into the most welcoming, multilayered malt-led flavours, all wrapped up by a firm, lingering bitterness.

THE STORY Smells have the ability to evoke powerful memories. And 4 Pines ESB is one that takes this writer instantly to a cosy corner table close to an ember-crackling log fire in an old, elegantly fading English pub, a pack of pork scratchings in one hand, a pint in the other, and an old chap thumbing the racing pages across the way.

It is the beer that captures the essence of an Extra Special Bitter better than any I have tasted in more than six years in Australia. This beer has brought on similar waves of nostalgia with other expat Brits to whom I have introduced it; it really does take you to the other side of the world with every sniff and taste. It is also something of a rarity in Australia: an English-style beer that resists the temptation to add a New World twist. Hopefully, it might inspire more brewers to do the same.

Brewer's food match
Richer meats, such as pork belly, duck, venison, moose or free range bison, or a good summer antipasto plate

Availability
Year round

Where to find it
National retailers, good independent bottle shops, on tap at selected venues

Brewery location
4F, 9–13 Winbourne Road, Brookvale, New South Wales

Cellar door
29/43–45 E Esplanade, Manly, New South Wales

Brewery website
www.4pinesbeer.com.au

Raging Bull
BOOTLEG BREWERY

 Robust porter/ strong dark ale 7.1% 7°C Brandy balloon

TASTING NOTES This strong ale pours an almost opaque, deep rusty-brown colour with a blood-red tinge and an off-white head. From start to finish, it's a luscious beast offering up raisins, treacle, berries, dark sugar, milk chocolate – even plums at the end.

THE STORY Even today, the WA beer scene retains an almost mythical status in the eastern states, as so little of it is ever seen outside its home state. Few breweries in the birthplace of craft beer in Australia package their beer; some rarely even sell beer outside theirown brewery, while most who do have bottled beer still refuse to send it across the Nullarbor.

One of the few beers to have fled the coop in the past is Bootleg's Raging Bull, a trophy-winning beer from Margaret River's oldest microbrewery. Part of the reason it was allowed to flee is that, as its name suggests, it is a beastly enough beer to survive the road trip east – a trip that, if made via unrefrigerated transport, is the equivalent of sending beer across the equator. As the Bootleg range has evolved in keeping with the changing marketplace, the Raging Bull has remained steadfastly the same: a minor Aussie craft beer classic as robust as the boxer whose nickname it shares.

Brewer's food match
Chocolate brownies

Availability
Year round

Where to find it
Good independent bottle shops in Victoria and Western Australia

Brewery and cellar door location
Puzey Road, Wilyabrup, Western Australia

Brewery website
www.bootlegbrewery.com.au

Seeing Double

BREWBOYS

 **Scottish 'wee heavy' peated** **8.0%**  **12-15°C** **Cognac or brandy balloon**

TASTING NOTES As with everything from Adelaide's Brewboys, this strong Scotch ale holds nothing back. One-tenth of the grain bill is peated distilling malt so it's distinctly smoky, but said smokiness blends nicely with fruity and rich caramel flavours. Full-bodied, creamy and warming, too.

THE STORY From the outside, it's easy to jump to the conclusion that the craft beer scene in South Australia is as sedate as the state's capital. The reality is that, certainly nowadays, there's a fair bit going on, with a number of breweries opening each year. It's just that most of the smaller ones are able to sell pretty much all of their beer within the state, and have no need to try and find stockists elsewhere.

Occasionally, the odd beer does break rank, as has been the case with Brewboys' Seeing Double. It's a beer that's like a microcosm of the brewery: a bit brash, a bit ballsy, a little rough around the edges and possessing a healthy disregard for conformity. Unlike most of their beers, there is no reference to head brewer Simon Sellick's love of high-octane machines, but it's no less revved up. It's a high-ABV Scotch ale featuring peated distilling malt, an ingredient that most brewers shun entirely. Those who do use it on occasion will usually keep it to just a tiny fraction of the grain bill, but here it makes up 10 per cent, creating one seriously smoky, yet smooth, mother. One to settle into after a dinner of haggis, tatties and neeps, perhaps.

Brewer's food match
Cheese platter, particularly with a big blue, dried pears and smoked meats

Availability
Available most of the year

Where to find it
Various independent bottle shops

Brewery and cellar door location
151 Regency Road, Croydon Park, South Australia

Brewery website
www.brewboys.com.au

Sparkling Ale
COOPERS BREWERY

 Sparkling ale   5.8%    6°C   **Coopers pint glass (roll bottle before serving)**

TASTING NOTES Cloudy to the point of murky, this iconic Australian classic has a unique mix of fruity esters that mingle with sweet, bready and grainy malts and lightly fruity old-school hops.

THE STORY As any student of craft beer in Australia knows, history began in 1983 when three friends in Fremantle decided enough was enough and began brewing beers for which the end goal was flavour and authenticity, not mere profit. It's a great story, but one that's not entirely true: the family-owned Coopers Brewery in South Australia was still struggling along, brewing its traditional English-inspired ales, even while every man and his dog was drinking nothing other than their home state brewery's version of fizzy yellow mediocrity.

Sparkling Ale was one of founder Thomas Cooper's first brews back in 1862 and, like its much more recently added little brother, Pale Ale, it's not going to blow the minds of the kids chasing wild adventures in beer today. But it remains an icon that's still welcomed at barbecues across the land, has lured countless people away from bland lagers – and doubtless still has thousands of unwitting converts lying ahead.

Brewer's food match
Spicy, barbecued, Italian or Asian-style foods

Availability
Year round

Where to find it
Most leading retailers and selected venues

Brewery and cellar door location
461 South Road, Regency Park, South Australia

Brewery website
www.coopers.com.au

Vintage Ale
COOPERS BREWERY

 Ale   7.5%   10°C   **Slender craft beer glass (roll bottle before serving)**

TASTING NOTES Designed for cellaring, this beer changes over time. Fresh, the 2013 upped the hopping stakes, with US hops creating hitherto unheard of aromas of citrus, melon and pine. As it ages, this rusty-coloured ale will become more a tale of rich fruity and caramelised malts and the unique characteristics of Coopers' yeast. It's gently warming from the relatively high booze content too.

THE STORY From the king of the vertical tasting in Australia, Coopers, this annual release is designed to be cellared for up to five years, although you will find people still hanging onto the first-ever release and bottles from every year since. It's becoming increasingly popular, usually at beer festivals or at special beer dinners, to line up several vintages of the same beer for a side-by-side comparison, and anyone wanting to take the concept to its limit in Australia can do so with Coopers Vintage Ale.

First brewed in 1998 and released annually ever since, it's a beer that you will find in steadily dwindling numbers in the collections of most avid – and long-in-the-tooth – beer aficionados around Australia. It tends to age gracefully and intriguingly, even if recent experience suggests that the first batches from the late 90s now share more in common with vinegar than beer. An enjoyable reminder that fresh need not always be best.

Brewer's food match
Hearty meat and poultry dishes, sweet desserts and strong cheeses

Availability
Limited annual release in July

Where to find it
Selected retailers and venues

Brewery and cellar door location
461 South Road, Regency Park, South Australia

Brewery website
www.coopers.com.au

Special Pale Ale
COWARAMUP BREWING COMPANY

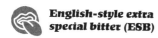 English-style extra special bitter (ESB)   5.4%  10-13°C   Traditional ale pint glass

TASTING NOTES Head brewer Jeremy Good's tipple of choice is a faithful re-creation of an English extra special bitter. There's a hint of floral hops alongside the biscuity malt aromas, with this rusty copper-coloured ale adding some fruitiness on the palate before a soft, earthy, persistent and lingering bitterness washes across the palate.

THE STORY It's not uncommon for people wanting to break into the brewing industry to donate their spare time to a favoured local micro in return for invaluable experience. But it's something you might expect of a teenager, or someone starting out in their working life – not so much from someone two decades into a career in IT. Yet that's what Jeremy Good started doing on weekends: offering his services for free to clean kegs and act as brewery dogsbody for WA's Feral Brewing. In return, head brewer Brendan Varis offered guidance as Jeremy moved from home-brewing IT guide to owner of his own brewery in the Margaret River region.

There, the expat Brit focuses predominantly on creating beer styles from his mother country, resisting any temptation to chase fads or experiment in favour of trying to perfect the handful of beers in his range. His pilsener (found elsewhere in this book) has taken the headlines, but it's with the traditional British ales that his heart lies, in particular this Special Pale Ale, inspired by the extra special bitters of his homeland.

Brewer's food match
Roast beef and Yorkshire pudding

Availability
Year round

Where to find it
Margaret River Hotel, Clancy's (City Beach and Dunsborough), Goodfella's

Cafe Restaurant Margaret River, El Rio Mexican

Brewery and cellar door location
229 North Treeton Road, Cowaramup, Western Australia

Brewery website
www.cowaramupbrewing.com.au

Moonshine

GRAND RIDGE BREWERY

 Dark Scotch ale 8.5% Serve cold and allow to warm up to 6-8°C to truly open up Brandy balloon

TASTING NOTES Like the same brewery's Supershine, this beer is like dessert in a glass. It's a strong Scotch ale that's a luxuriant, mouth-coating, sweet treat and is all about burnt toffee, treacle, caramel and plums.

THE STORY This luscious, mountainous monument to the wonders of rich, sweet malts in beer is worthy of a place in any list on the strength of the bottle contents alone. But, more than that, it is a beer with its own unique spot in Australian craft beer history, too. As one of the first beers released by Grand Ridge, the Mirboo North brewery that is the oldest existing micro in Victoria, it is one of the longest continuously brewed beers in the country.

Controversy surrounded its early days. Brewed from a wort with an original gravity of 1080, it was originally called just that, 1080, and came with a label bearing that name. It was a name shared with a popular brand of poison, something that didn't go down too well with the powers-that-be. Thus 1080 was no more and Moonshine was born, a beer that, a quarter-century later, still goes down well late at night, particularly with a rich pudding or a hefty chunk of blue cheese.

Brewer's food match
Sticky date pudding with burnt caramel

Availability
Year round

Where to find it
Brewery Direct, Dan Murphy's, First Choice and all good independent bottle shops

Brewery and cellar door location
1 Baromi Road, Mirboo North, Victoria

Brewery website
www.grand-ridge.com.au

ESB

HARGREAVES HILL

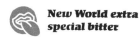 **New World extra special bitter** **5.2%** **6-8°C** **Tulip glass**

TASTING NOTES This New World take on the classic British ESB style is Hargreaves Hill's star beer. It takes the robust malt backbone that you would find in beers from the old country and adds aromatic New World hops to give it a hugely appealing passionfruit aroma.

THE STORY This is the beer that made a name for Yarra Valley brewery Hargreaves Hill. Head brewer Simon Walkenhorst took a traditional ESB and, instead of combining it with the more earthy hop varieties you might find in the UK, spruced it up with a far more flamboyant American variety not long landed in Australia. Given brewers' predilection for mixing and matching every conceivable style within the same beer these days, the mere use of New World hops in an Old World style seems rather matter of fact today.

Yet if this ESB's appeal lay solely in its novelty factor, it would not have enjoyed the longevity it has, nor indeed become the favoured tipple of so many drinkers. Its ongoing success comes down to the fact that, like pretty much every beer released by Hargreaves Hill, it is immaculately conceived – and darn delicious, too.

Brewer's food match
Pepper-crusted venison

Availability
Year round

Where to find it
All good craft beer bottle shops and venues

Brewery location
60/64–86 Beresford Road, Lilydale, Victoria

Cellar door
25 Bell Street, Yarra Glen, Victoria

Brewery website
www.hargreaveshill.com.au

Nut Brown Ale

HOLGATE BREWHOUSE

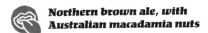 Northern brown ale, with Australian macadamia nuts 5.3%  6-8°C Nonic or jar

TASTING NOTES This is a deeply dark, rich and rounded comforter for the warmer months, featuring layers of luscious chocolate and much toasty nuttiness (thanks to the addition of roasted macadamia nuts) tied up with an earthy, drying bitterness.

THE STORY Holgate founder Paul Holgate was inspired to become a brewer by experiences holidaying in the UK and the US in the 90s. As such, his brewery's range features a smattering of British and American styles and, when it came time to mark Holgate's tenth anniversary, it was to the UK he looked once more. At a time in the country's beer revolution when local brewers seemed to favour marking anniversaries with beers crammed to the gills (and beyond) with hops, or beers registering somewhat unhinged levels of alcohol content, he took a rather different approach. Roasted macadamia nuts were added to a beer that already had plenty of depth, thanks to a complex malt bill, resulting in a smooth, rich-yet-quaffable wintry ale that proved so popular, it has returned every year since.

Brewer's food match
Pork belly, roast suckling pig, roast duck

Availability
Seasonal

Where to find it
Limited to specialty bottle shops when in season

Brewery and cellar door location
79 High Street, Woodend, Victoria

Brewery website
www.holgatebrewhouse.com

Old Admiral

LORD NELSON BREWERY HOTEL

 Dark ale **6.1%** **4–6°C** **Pint**

TASTING NOTES This English-style strong ale is the pick of the Lord Nelson permanent range. It pours a deep brown and offers up a wealth of flavours and aromas. There are sweet malts of the chocolate, caramel and treacle variety and plenty of dark fruits, too: plums and raisins like rich fruit pudding, backed up by its gently warming alcohol.

THE STORY The Lord Nelson Brewery Hotel in The Rocks in Sydney is not only one of the finest pubs in the whole of Australia, it's also one of the few survivors from the very first wave of microbreweries in the 80s. More than a quarter-century ago, Blair Hayden, not long back from living and working in the UK, took over what is the oldest licensed hotel in the city and started brewing beers based on the real ales he had enjoyed overseas. The brewery setup is one of the most unique in Australia, wending its way ingeniously through various rooms and spaces in the pub's cellar.

For the most part, the Lord Nelson's beers are only found on tap at the pub itself, although two – the Three Sheets Australian Pale Ale and Old Admiral Ale – are packaged offsite and available widely. The Three Sheets is the best known and the biggest seller, but the Old Admiral is a better representation of what the Lord Nelson is all about.

Brewer's food match
Australian aged cheddar or Italian Parmigiano-Reggiano; grass-fed rib eye with truffle butter; flourless chocolate cake; ale-poached pears with King Island cream

Availability
Year round

Where to find it
Quality bars and restaurants; independent bottle shops

Brewery and cellar door location
19 Kent Street, The Rocks, New South Wales

Brewery website
www.lordnelsonbrewery.com

Challenger

MASH BREWING

 English IPA 5.8%  6-8°C Pint

TASTING NOTES This is a glistening amber English IPA that is centred around the distinct orange marmalade characteristics often found in the beers that inspired it. There's plenty of rich caramel too, but really it's about that marmalade, from the aroma through to the almost resinous hops on the palate.

THE STORY The parting impression following my first visit to Mash Brewing in the Swan Valley a few years ago was that it was a place with a fantastic venue and setup that lacked the beers to match. Soon afterwards, the appointment of head brewer Charlie Hodgson put that to rights, with a redesigned core range supplemented by frequently intriguing, consistently high-quality seasonals. One of those,

Challenger, has proven so successful that it lives on and is now brewed both in WA and at Mash's joint venture, 3 Ravens, in Melbourne. As with all of the brewery's seasonal releases, it has plenty to offer without going overboard, in keeping with Charlie's goal of achieving complexity with balance.

Brewer's food match
Rib eye oven-roasted steak, lamb rack

Availability
Year round

Where to find it
The Sail and Anchor (hand pump), select Dan Murphy's stores in Perth and Melbourne, Liquor Barons Bayswater and Morley, Cellarbrations Carlisle and other select bottle shops in Perth

Brewery and cellar door location
10250 West Swan Road, Henley Brook, Swan Valley, Western Australia

Brewery website
www.mashbrewing.com

Irish Red Ale

MORRISON BREWERY

 Irish red ale   5.1%    10°C   Pint

TASTING NOTES This ruddy red number from Launceston's Morrison Brewery is all about the malt. A smooth and balanced medium-bodied beer that offers up toffee, caramel and toasted malt flavours, with just enough bitterness to tidy up the back-end.

THE STORY Every young home brewer would like a family like Paul Morrison's. Once Paul showed a talent for brewing by achieving success with beers entered into competitions in his home state of Tasmania and across the Bass Strait in Melbourne, his dad suggested stepping up and brewing them commercially. They installed a small microbrewery in a warehouse in Launceston in late 2011, with Paul, his wife, father, sister and her husband all involved in the business in one way or another.

His first beer was poured at Hobart's iconic New Sydney Hotel, and he now supplies a number of venues around the state capital, as well as occupying a handful of taps elsewhere in the state. Less than two years after opening the brewery, he was able to quit his job at an orchard in order to focus on brewing full-time, with a focus that is trained mainly on creating traditional British and Irish ales.

Brewer's food match
Game meats

Availability
Year round

Where to find it
Tasmanian BWS outlets, Liquor Stax, Big Bargain bottle shops, various

independent bottle shops and bars throughout Tasmania.

Brewery location
Launceston, Tasmania

Brewery website
www.morrisonbrewery.com.au

Punch & Judy
MURRAY'S CRAFT BREWING

 Bitter/amber ale   **3.9%**  **8-12°C**   **Nonic pint glass**

TASTING NOTES The taste of an English pub beer garden via New Zealand on a mild summer's afternoon, this copper-coloured bitter matches the rich, nutty malt profile of classic English ales with fruity Kiwi hop aromas to create a truly sessionable, thirst-quenching beer.

THE STORY There is a growing and welcome trend in the Australian beer world that sees brewers striving to create full-flavoured mid-strength beers with enough character to appeal to craft beer lovers. One of the first to attempt it and nail it was Murray's. The Port Stephens brewery's Punch & Judy takes a lead from the UK, where flavoursome, hoppy real ales around about the 3.5 to 4 per cent mark are commonplace rather than a rarity. The British influence is most clearly seen in the malt structure, with the hops of a much more New World nature thanks to head brewer Shawn Sherlock's enduring love affair with Kiwi hops.

It's a fine beer in any format, but if you get the chance to sample it poured from a hand pump at one of the few, but slowly growing, number of venues to have one, grab it with both hands as that is when it really shines.

Brewer's food match
Ploughman's lunch

Availability
Year round

Where to find it
Good craft venues on draught; BWS and good independent bottle shops Australia-wide

Brewery and cellar door location
3443 Nelson Bay Road, Bobs Farm, New South Wales

Brewery website
www.murraysbrewingco.com.au

Redoak Bitter
REDOAK

 British bitter **3.5%** **4°C**  **Ale or pint glass**

TASTING NOTES A beautifully balanced mix of Old World and New World, this amber-coloured bitter boasts a surprisingly full flavour for a mere 3.5 per cent beer, combining rich caramel malts with citrusy Australian hops to perfection.

THE STORY Sydney's Redoak has been creating award-winning beers for a decade. Its beers have collected some of the most prestigious trophies in the world, with head brewer David Hollyoak usually entering beers in competitions in the countries where those beer styles originated and frequently beating the home team at their own game.

Yet, despite all the baubles and gongs, he and sister Janet have struggled to secure taps in their home city, highlighting the challenges faced by small brewers trying to break the market. Thankfully, in 2013, Sydney started showing signs that its beer and bar culture is changing, as more venues embraced good beer and more quality microbreweries started out. Perhaps it means this bitter, as fine a session beer as you'll find in Australia, will have more luck. That said, it's always worth a trip to the Redoak Boutique Beer Cafe anyway, where you can sample it alongside more than a dozen other excellent Redoak drops.

Brewer's food match
Game and Asian-inspired dishes

Availability
Year round

Where to find it
Select bottle shops

Cellar door location
201 Clarence Street, Sydney, New South Wales

Brewery website
www.redoak.com.au

Kentish Ale

SEVEN SHEDS

 Kentish ale   5.2%   6-8°C   Straight pint glass

TASTING NOTES An excellent local example of a classic English pale ale, this is a bright copper-coloured beer with a white head, with lifted floral and peachy hop aromas that sit delicately on the palate. Sweet biscuit and caramel malts are followed by a soft, earthy bitterness in what's a great display of English and Tasmanian hops.

THE STORY For a quarter century, long before he took his home-brewing skills into the commercial realm, expat Kiwi Willie Simpson was Australia's foremost (at times, only) beer writer. He wrote books and a regular column for the *Sydney Morning Herald* (which he only retired in 2013) before setting up Seven Sheds in Tasmania to effectively walk the walk.

He has done so with a series of beers that are frequently fiercely traditional and occasionally highly experimental, although, even in the latter case, usually inspired by milestone moments in beer's long history. His flagship beer falls firmly in the former category, with the Kentish Ale taking its name from the region of northwest Tasmania where the brewery is based, but also doffing its cap to England, the country whose pale ales this beer recreates with aplomb.

Brewer's food match
Rabbit pie and chips

Availability
Year round

Where to find it
Selected Tasmanian outlets, on tap at the Stanley Hotel, Mole Creek Hotel,

Cradle Mountain Chateau, Lark's Distillery Cafe (Hobart)

Brewery and cellar door location
22 Crockers Street, Railton, Tasmania

Brewery website
www.sevensheds.com

Hop Ale
YOUNG HENRYS

 **Australian IPA**   **6.0%**   **Cold or room temperature**   **IPA glass**

TASTING NOTES The pick of the Young Henrys core range takes a classic English IPA as its starting point, with a rich, dense and hearty caramel malt body. It then gives it a serious Aussie working over, with vast quantities of multiple local hop varieties adding big citrus aromas and deep, complex, grapefruit-dominated hop flavours. Little wonder the head brewer has been invited to create real ale versions of his beers in the UK.

THE STORY In its relatively short history, Newtown's Young Henrys has achieved a phenomenal amount. It has secured taps in seemingly every venue in the surrounding suburbs, become a vibrant community hub, collaborated with artists, roasters, radio stations and You Am I, sponsored events and created beers with mussels, clams, agave nectar, vanilla and more besides. So selecting this relatively tame (by their standards) take on an English IPA may seem surprisingly mundane. However, it's one of few Young Henrys beers available year round; it's a damn fine take on the style; and it can also be found here and there on hand pump, a rare experience in Australia and one that, in the case of the Hop Ale, should be snapped up at every opportunity.

Brewer's food match
Anything with the words 'roast pork' attached

Availability
Year round

Where to find it
On tap and in bottle shops in and around Sydney's inner west

Brewery and cellar door location
76 Wilford Street, Newtown, New South Wales

Brewery website
www.younghenrys.com

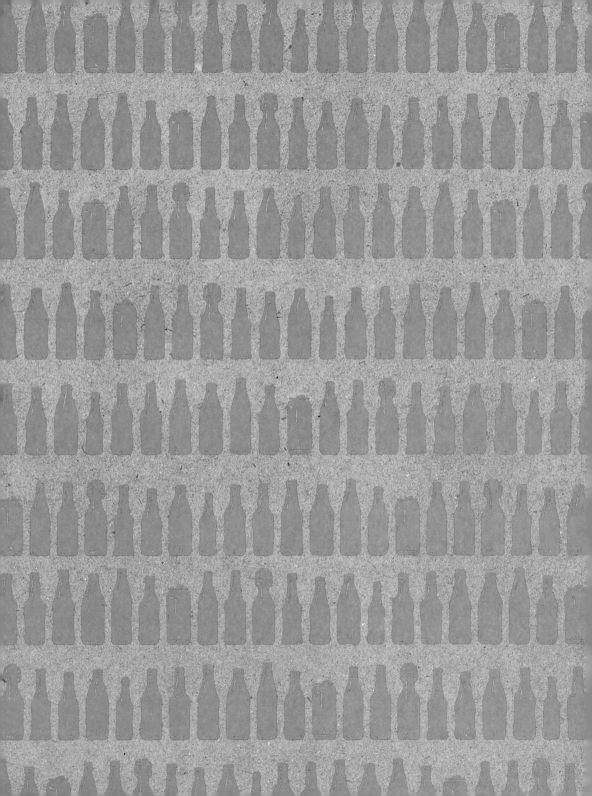

RED
AND
AMBER
ALES

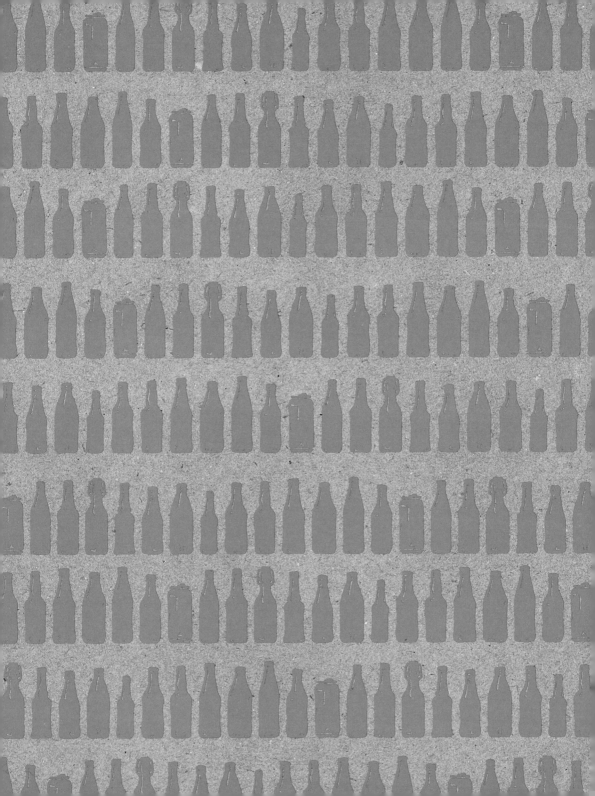

Red and Amber Ales

As the title suggests, the beers gathered together in this chapter are united more by their hue than any other characteristic. And, for the most part, there is no great historical heritage attached to the terms 'red ale' or 'amber ale'.

There are exceptions, such as the Flanders Red style (see the Belgian Styles chapter), a unique sour and fruity ale that originates in Belgium but is practically non-existent within the entire output of Australia's brewers.

More recently, American amber ales have become acknowledged as a category. In many ways, these beers are simply a step up from American pale ales. Usually they share those beers' citrusy hop aromas, but are, of course, darker in colour and possess a more strident malt character, typically sweeter and of a caramel nature.

It is these American influences that have proved increasingly popular with Australian brewers. The majority of beers contained in this section would fall under the American amber banner through their combination of upfront hop aromas, rich malt flavours and distinct bitterness.

There are others, however, that reflect contemporary brewers' affection for experimentation and creativity, and the merging of traditional beer styles. A growing number are tagging their beers as 'India red ale', 'red IPA' or even 'amber IPA'. In many ways, it's like a code that can be easily deciphered. Whenever you see the word 'India' attached to a beer style, it refers back to India pale ales, so expect higher levels of hop aroma, hop flavour and hop-derived bitterness.

When 'IPA' is used in conjunction with a colour, such as red, amber, black or white, it is describing the colour of the beer; from that, deductions can usually be made as to the flavour as well. In red or amber beers, the drinker can expect richer, sweeter malt flavours: caramel, toffee, chocolate, nut, sometimes even vanilla.

With the red and amber ales that follow, their colouring is achieved purely through the brewer's choice of malt. The malts have been kilned until they are of a darker hue than the pale malts used as the basis for the vast majority of beers, and can deliver red, amber and ruddy colouring as well as the aforementioned sweeter flavours, even when used as a small percentage of the overall grain bill.

TOP OF THE HOPS

RIVERSIDE BREWING 44 AMERICAN AMBER
DAINTON FAMILY BREWING RED EYE RYE
WAYWARD BREWING COMPANY CHARMER INDIA RED ALE

Grizz

2 BROTHERS BREWERY

 American amber 5.7% 4°C Conical pint

TASTING NOTES Inspired by Mack and Jack's Amber from Washington State, a favourite of 2 Brothers brewer Andrew Ong, this fuses punchy, fruity hops from the Pacific Northwest with rich, chewy caramel malts in a big and boisterous yet balanced beer.

THE STORY Given that Andrew and David Ong fell in love with good beer while working in America – one as a bullet-dodging physio in the Bronx, the other as a number-crunching aeronautical engineer in Seattle – and bought their brewery from a former brewpub in New York's Times Square, it's fitting that there has been an American theme running through many of their beers. From the start, their American brown ale, Growler,

has been a mainstay of their range, although in recent times it's Grizz that seems to have found greater favour in beer fanciers' hearts.

Almost imperceptibly, its furry orange tap head has begun appearing on the bars of crafty and not-so-crafty bars across the country, giving the impression that Fozzie Bear has escaped from the Muppets and is leaving calling cards wherever he stops for a refresher. It's understandable, as the beer's combination of enticing New World hops and chewy malts offers plenty of enticement to come back for more.

Brewer's food match
Grilled salmon, Dungeness crab

Availability
Year round

Where to find it
McCoppins (Fitzroy), Grain and Grape (Moorabbin), Valley Cellars (Moonee Ponds)

Brewery and cellar door location
4 Joyner Street, Moorabbin, Victoria

Brewery website
www.2brothers.com.au

Red Eye Rye

DAINTON FAMILY BREWERY

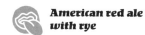 American red ale with rye   4.8%   4°C   Tulip glass

TASTING NOTES It's a beer with a shopping list of hops and malts that's a sure sign of a home brewer turned pro, but one that's carried off with aplomb. The seven malts and six hops combine seamlessly for a fruity, spicy, malty, impeccably clean debut from Dan Dainton.

THE STORY The name 'Dainton Family Brewery' sounds rather quaint, bringing to mind images of John-Boy and Jim-Bob. The label artwork and messages scrawled on the sides of the early releases from the brewing company formed by brewer Dan Dainton alongside his father and sister suggest a rather more colourful – sinister, even – connotation to the name. Like the scribbles of Danish gypsy brewer Beer Here, the twisted, demonic images are certainly eye catching; thankfully, the beers inside, at least going by the early releases, are as worthy of attention. This, his first release after leaving Holgate Brewhouse, was as good a debut as any in 2013, an immaculately conceived beer with layers of both hop and malt character for the drinker to unravel, all wrapped up in a clean and balanced ale that leaves you wanting more.

Brewer's food match
Spicy chicken or vintage cheddar

Availability
Year round

Where to find it
Purvis, Slow Beer, McCoppins and all good craft beer venues

Brewery location
Kialla, Victoria

Brewery website
www.daintonfamilybrewing.com.au

Phoenix Imperial Red Ale

HARGREAVES HILL

 Imperial red ale   9.3%  8-10°C   Brandy snifter

TASTING NOTES Opulence in beer form, this gleaming, viscous red ale positively glows in the glass and clings to its sides as it makes its way mouthwards, bearing gifts of pine, clotted cream toffee, raisins, marmalade, butter biscuits, muscat and more. Much more.

THE STORY The original Hargreaves Hill brewery was destroyed in the Black Saturday fires that swept across Victoria in 2009. The support of friends within the local beer industry kept the business going, with fellow brewers inviting founder Simon Walkenhorst to brew on their equipment while he and wife Beth pondered their next move.

Once they had found a new brewery site, they created a beer to mark their rebirth. The name, Phoenix, was an obvious choice; the style, an imperial red ale, was less so as it was one rarely, if ever, attempted by Australian brewers at that point. The resulting beer has only been brewed twice, in keeping with Hargreaves Hill's laid-back approach to all things, but has achieved minor cult status nonetheless. It is one of the most gloriously decadent and luxuriant beers you can get your hands on, making it fit and proper that each of its weighty, 750 ml, individually numbered bottles comes complete with a hand-dipped wax seal.

Brewer's food match
Duck

Availability
Annual – limited release of bottles and kegs

Where to find it
Selected bottle shops and venues

Brewery location
60/64–86 Beresford Road, Lilydale, Victoria

Cellar door
25 Bell Street, Yarra Glen, Victoria

Brewery website
www.hargreaveshill.com.au

Hopped Out Red

KAIJU! BEER (FORMERLY MONSTER MASH)

 American red ale 6.4% 6-8°C Spiegelau IPA glass

TASTING NOTES The second beer from the artists formerly known as Monster Mash even *looks* hoppy from a distance, with its reddish-brown body seeming to have the faintest resinous green hue. Its hop aromas – grassy, tropical, piny – don't hit you alone, as there's a fair whack of caramel sweetness in there. The hops and malt go to battle over your palate too, before this decidedly hearty beer ends with a decidedly hearty bitterness.

THE STORY Their first release (as Monster Mash) was a 9.1 per cent, hopped to the eyeballs and beyond double IPA (see elsewhere in this book). And, as if to prove that they meant business, when it came to releasing their second beer, the brothers behind Kaiju! (Japanese for 'strange creature') opted for another heavy blast of heady hops.

With not even a single hop pellet or flower used early in the brewing process, when they are traditionally added to create bitterness, it's a credit to just how many hops are added at the end of the brew that this full-flavoured red ale still packs a significant bitter punch. With a similarly hopped-up IPA released as beer number three, one suspects we needn't hold our breath for an approachable golden ale or Kolsch from these guys any time soon. In fact, when asked why their opening salvo featured two such in-your-face releases, the answer was simple: 'We chose the beers we're good at brewing.' And, presumably, the ones they like to drink.

Brewer's food match
Washed-rind cheeses such as Taleggio

Availability
Year round (limited)

Where to find it
Slowbeer, Small Patch, The Park Hotel Werribee, Caulfield Cellars, McCoppins

Brewery location
Derrimut (Cavalier), Victoria

Brewery website
www.kaijubeer.com.au

Amber Ale
KILLER SPROCKET

 Amber ale   **4.8%**    **3-6°C**   **Shaker pint**

TASTING NOTES This is a debut beer that left nothing in the locker room. More than anything, this deep amber ale is all about the malt, running the confectionery store gamut from chocolate and toffee to fruit and nut.

THE STORY One can't help but see the name 'Killer Sprocket' and wonder what inspired such an unusual and colourful moniker. When you learn that the brewing company's founder is also a standup comedian, you just know the reason is going to be good. Somewhat disappointingly, it turns out that it was merely a name given to a reporting database by said brewer/comedian Sean Ryan when he was working for an insurance company.

Thankfully, since entering the beer world with his wife and brewing partner, Andrea, disappointment has been kept at bay as drinkers have been treated to this delicious debut and a quirky follow-up, the smoky Bandit, featuring peated distilling malt. Demand has spread quickly outside their home state of Victoria. (As for the database, it grew too large, began crashing government systems and was decommissioned – but the name lives on.)

Brewer's food match
Drinkable with everything, but especially creamy, biscuit or chocolate desserts

Availability
Year round

Where to find it
Victoria, Queensland and Newcastle

Brewery location
Derrimut, Victoria

Brewery website
www.killersprocket.com.au

Archie's Red Ale

MISMATCH BREWING COMPANY

 Red ale   **5.0%**    **5-8°C**   **Tulip glass**

TASTING NOTES For their first release, these self-proclaimed 'brewing nomads' chose a style they felt was missing in their local South Australian market. They did a fine job too, with this tidy dark-red beer combining aromatic, citrusy American hops, dark caramel flavours and a firm bitterness.

THE STORY When Little Creatures was taken over by Lion in 2012, there was an exodus of sales staff. Most of them soon cropped up at many of the fast-expanding microbreweries across the country, ready to help the next wave grow.

One rep, however, headed to the UK to study brewing instead. Upon returning to Australia, Ewan Brewerton, who had previously worked for SA's McLaren Vale Brewing as well, founded Mismatch Brewing with a few mates and became the first brewing company to sign up to use Adelaide's Big Shed Brewing, a new communal facility opened to give SA brewers a means of entering the brewing world without buying their own gear. Ewan kicked off his venture with Archie's Red Ale, a well-judged red ale designed to fill a gap in the local market. It's not named after a famous cartoon redhead, but a mate who had recently beaten cancer.

Brewer's food match
Anything with spice, eg. Indian and Thai

Availability
Year round

Where to find it
South Australian independent bottle shops and selected bars

Brewery location
Big Shed Brewing, 2/13 Brandwood Street, Royal Park, South Australia

Brewery website
www.mismatchbrewing.com.au

Hightail Ale

MOUNTAIN GOAT

 Amber ale 4.5% 5°C English pint glass

TASTING NOTES After sixteen years of refinement, the Hightail achieves a perfect blend of citrus and floral hops with nutty and caramel malts, all tied up with just the right amount of bitterness. A timeless Aussie classic.

THE STORY You can use Mountain Goat's Hightail as a barometer for the evolution of craft beer in Australia. It was the Richmond brewer's first release back in 1997, based on head brewer Dave Bonighton's favourite home-brew recipe. Inspired by his time living and drinking beer in the US, it was designed to be a beer that he and business partner Cam Hines would want to drink themselves; a beer they couldn't find amid the sea of mediocrity that was on offer in Australia at the time. It was also designed to shake things up, to shock drinkers with the boldness of its rich toffee and chocolate malt character, upfront hop aromas and finishing bitterness.

Today, it remains the brewery's flagship (although long overtaken by Steam Ale in terms of sales) and, while constantly evolving, is essentially the same beast. It has also been the basis for the beers with which they marked their tenth and fifteenth anniversaries: the Double Hightail and Triple Hightail, which took the basic recipe and doubled, then tripled, the hops and malt.

Brewer's food match
Roast lamb and vegies

Availability
Year round

Where to find it
Bottle shops Australia-wide

Brewery and cellar door location
80 North Street, Richmond, Victoria

Brewery website
www.goatbeer.com.au

India Red Ale

PRANCING PONY BREWERY

 American imperial red ale **7.9%** **8°C** **Tulip glass**

TASTING NOTES The first 'thoroughbred' release from this new SA brewery would score highly for presentation in dressage, thanks to its deep red colour and dense, lingering head that coats the glass. Tropical, herbal hops merge with caramel atop a full-bodied beer with enough biscuity, toasty malt to carry off the high level of bitterness.

THE STORY It's impossible to discover anything about the Adelaide Hills' Prancing Pony Brewery, whether from chatting to someone who knows their beers or visiting their brewery bar, without hearing about their 'fire brewing'. They chose to make it a point of difference when launching, based on the fact that their brewhouse is effectively a ten-times scaled-up replica of brewer Frank Samson's home brew setup, with a large flame burner in its base. The idea is that it lends the beer greater qualities of caramelisation.

Certainly, a colourful (and colourfully presented) range of beers has helped Prancing Pony enjoy a flying start that has seen them take over a second warehouse unit and significantly expand their cellar door offering within their first twelve months. By 2014, they were eyeing up a much larger venue and a bigger brewery; one with a giant flame in its base, of course.

Brewer's food match
Barossa Berkshire pork belly with ginger and orange sauce

Availability
Year round

Where to find it
Most independent bottle shops in South Australia

Brewery location
U3/4 Simper Crescent, Mount Barker, South Australia

Brewery website
www.prancingponybrewery.com.au

44 American Amber Ale

RIVERSIDE BREWING COMPANY

 American amber ale   **6.5%**   **6-8°C**   **Tulip glass**

TASTING NOTES This is a riotous collision of mounds of rich biscuit, toffee, burnt caramel and toasted malts with a wall of boisterous American hops in which no one wins. Except you, the drinker.

THE STORY It's funny how some beers just seem to resonate, to achieve cult status almost overnight. Since launching in 2012, Parramatta's Riverside Brewing has released some fantastic, critically and publicly acclaimed beers. But it's the 44 that all the cool kids seem to be drinking around Sydney's growing number of craft-supporting small bars.

It's not the most common of styles, and this is a no-holds-barred take on an American amber to boot, yet it appears to be on every other tap in the city's best venues. What's more, the people behind those taps, as well as seemingly half of the state's brewers, are rarely found without a 44 in their hands either.

Brewer's food match
Strong-flavoured foods, such as smoked beef brisket

Availability
Year round

Where to find it
Currently Sydney and Newcastle only; Melbourne and Brisbane soon

Brewery and cellar door location
2 North Rocks Road, North Parramatta, New South Wales

Brewery website
www.riversidebrewing.com.au

Sunset Ale

TWO BIRDS BREWING

 Red/amber ale 4.6% 6°C *Spiegelau classic stem glass*

TASTING NOTES As a former winemaker turned brewer, Jayne Lewis seeks balance more than anything in her beers, and that's the case here, with enticing tropical aromas and flavours melding happily with soft biscuit and toffee malts in a well-rounded red ale.

THE STORY Though she would never admit it, Two Birds' Jayne Lewis is as close as the Australian craft beer world has to a star. Ever present at festivals with 'Other Bird', Danielle Allen, and a voracious and passionate advocate for better beer both within and outside the craft beer world, the former Little Creatures, Matilda Bay and Mountain Goat brewer also works tirelessly to promote the role of women within brewing.

When it comes to beer, Two Birds is based around approachability and sessionability, an ethos that has seen them achieve remarkable success across the country in a short space of time. With their own brewery in the Melbourne suburb of Spotswood opening in 2014, it's a success that is sure to grow.

Brewer's food match
Duck, goat's cheese, roasted beetroot

Availability
Year round

Where to find it
Vintage Cellars, First Choice, all quality independent bottle shops

Brewery and cellar door location
136 Hall Street, Spotswood, Victoria

Brewery website
www.twobirdsbrewing.com.au

Charmer India Red Ale

WAYWARD BREWING COMPANY

 India red ale **5.0%**  **6°C** **Tulip glass**

TASTING NOTES This is a beer that holds back nothing on the malt or hops front and achieves a perfect balance between the two. It pours a deep russet colour and gives off a full, rounded aroma of orange and toffee. In the mouth it's similarly smooth and rounded, with some toasted malts as well as the toffee proving ideal company for those fruity hops.

THE STORY After fourteen years as a home brewer, expat American Peter Philip decided to take his beers into the public sphere. And, for the discerning beer drinkers of Sydney, it was a fine decision. Operating as a gypsy brewer – brewing on other people's equipment, usually that of his former work colleague–turned–brewer Dave Padden at Riverside Brewing – he has released a diverse range of beers in a short space of time, all of a consistently high standard. The Charmer was his first release and is a fine flagship for the Wayward brand, enjoying success in the eyes of qualified beer judges and Joe Public alike. Hopefully, he will secure his own brewery site, as the watermark for Australian brewing overall will rise if he is able to dedicate his life full time to brewing beer and leave e-commerce behind.

Brewer's food match
Grilled meat; steak, pork ribs, beef ribs with spicy and sticky barbecue sauce

Availability
Year round

Where to find it
Limited bottle supply, good availability on draught at craft beer establishments in Sydney, occasionally available in Melbourne and Brisbane; Harts Pub, The Australian Hotel, The Wild Rover, The Pumphouse, Spooning Goats, The Empire Hotel, Chippendale Hotel, Forest Lodge Hotel

Brewery location
Gypsy brewed

Cellar door
Batch Brewing Co, 44 Sydenham Road, Marrickville, New South Wales

Brewery website
www.waywardbrewing.com.au

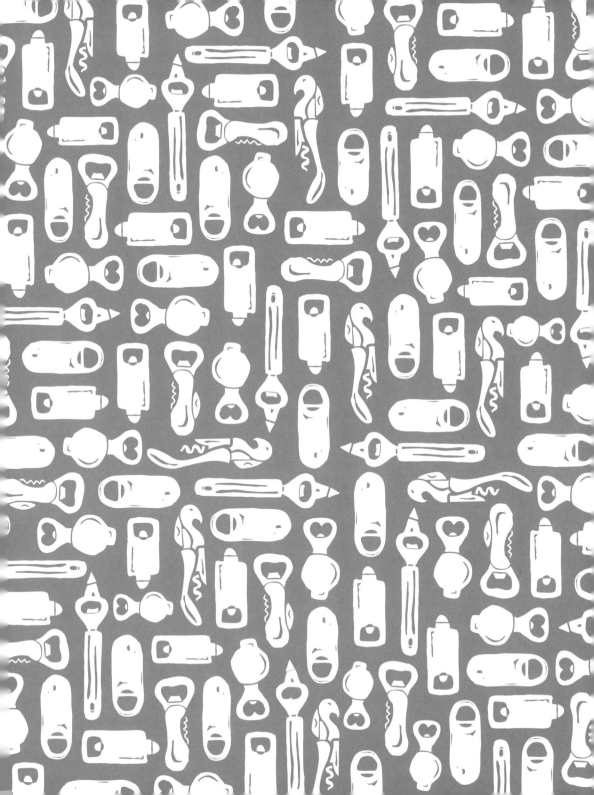

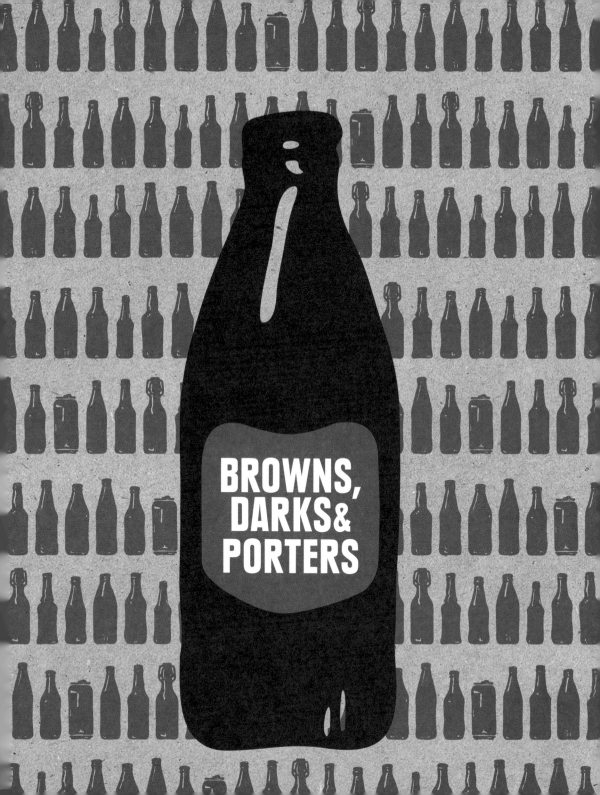

BROWNS,
DARKS &
PORTERS

Browns, Darks and Porters

Over the coming pages you will find beers that fall into two main categories - brown ale and porter - as well as their American-inspired reinterpretations. They are styles that share many common characteristics; indeed, at the upper, darker end of the brown ale style there is little to distinguish between them and many bearing the 'porter' handle.

As for 'dark ales', it is a broad-brush term that could cover brown ales, porters, even stouts. In Australia, the few that carry the name, such as Coopers Dark Ale, and the White Rabbit Dark Ale featured here, could as easily be called brown ales. To muddy the water a little further, you can find beers, usually in England, described as brown porters…

The origins of both brown ales and porters are found in the UK. Browns come in two main variants: the Northern English brown and Southern English brown. Both share many characteristics, however, in that they are brown in colour, with the former usually lighter in hue than the latter. Their flavours and aromas are predominantly derived from the brewer's choice of malt rather than hops. Expect malt sweetness and anything from milk chocolate and vanilla to toffee, cocoa and coffee, sometimes with fruity elements, such as raisins or plums, apparent too.

American brown ales do what you would expect from American brewers: they take the English originals and turn them up to 11. Drinkers can expect fuller, richer malt flavours, slightly higher alcohol content and the addition, in many cases, of more noticeable, often citrusy or piny, hop aromas and flavours.

Porter is a style with one of the most colourful histories of all British beers; indeed, it's a history that one could never do full justice in a few paragraphs. Typically darker and higher in alcohol content than English brown ales, their origins can be traced to early eighteenth-century London. They are origins that, like the India pale ale, have sprouted stories of dubious authenticity, such as one that claims the style's name comes from the drinkers that originally enjoyed it: the porters who quaffed it at the Blue Last, a pub pouring a dark ale brewed at the Bell Brewhouse.

The beer that came to be known as porter was typically a blend of several darker beers, mixed by publicans from multiple casks, due to the varied strength and maturity of beers that would arrive from the brewery. Brewers, most notably Ralph Harwood of the Bell Brewhouse, began blending beers before selling them to publicans, with these early porters usually brown, smoky and highly hopped.

The popularity of these beers coincided with the Industrial Revolution in the UK. Huge new breweries making use of new technologies emerged, signalling a shift to modern, large-scale commercial brewing, and began sending their beers across the UK and Ireland. Later, porters became popular in the early days of the United States and were also sent to Britain's colonies. When Tasmanian brewery Seven Sheds decided to re-create the journey of the first beers sent from the UK to Australia, head brewer Willie Simpson decided it would be porter that would fill the oak barrels that would spend two months traversing the Bass Strait back and forth.

By the early twentieth century, the style had declined dramatically in popularity. Once more, it was left to the new wave of craft brewers in the US to bring it back towards the end of the century. They did so with beers that are usually around 6 per cent in alcohol content and dominated by rich chocolate flavours and aromas, often with hints of vanilla, treacle, dark fruits, a touch of coffee and sometimes even leather or smokiness. Sometimes New World brewers will ramp up the hopping regime late in the brewing process to add citrusy or tropical fruit aromas, although most porter brewers in Australia resist this temptation.

Rather, when they do stray from the line it tends to be away from hoppiness or bitterness and towards sweetness and lusciousness. Within this section you will find a milk porter and one that uses cocoa and vanilla to create a dessert like richness, while there has been the occasional limited release imperial porter too, with notable recent examples from Holgate Brewhouse and Nail Brewing.

Interestingly, I have heard publicans in Australia claim on more than one occasion that if they were to change the name on a tap to say 'stout' instead of 'porter', sales would increase dramatically.

As with porters, so with brown ales in Australia. Despite a willingness to follow the American lead when it comes to pales, IPAs, reds and ambers, for the most part locally brewed brown ales are far more traditional and British in conception. There are exceptions, including the boldly hopped inclusions from Murray's and Prickly Moses in this chapter, but generally it's an area where the malts are allowed to take centre stage.

Note: there is also a style of beer called 'Baltic porter' that originates in Eastern Europe. These were based on imperial stouts but typically used lager yeasts or ale yeasts fermented at cool temperatures. There is one featured in this book and, after discussion with its brewer, you will find it in the chapter on lagers.

TOP OF THE HOPS ✪

MORNINGTON PENINSULA BREWERY BROWN ALE
THE LITTLE BREWING COMPANY WICKED ELF PORTER
HOLGATE BREWHOUSE TEMPTRESS

Staircase Porter
BRIGHT BREWERY

 Robust porter   5.7%   7–8°C  British pint glass

TASTING NOTES Bright's Staircase has a lovely, rich brown colour and serves up a balance of sweeter malts – toffee and milk chocolate – with those of a darker nature – bitter cocoa and roast coffee – that makes for a rather tasty package.

THE STORY From day one, Bright Brewery was blessed. Nestled in the heart of the Victorian High Country, it is surrounded by towering tree-studded mountains and sits just a skip and a jump away from the edge of the Ovens River. It's unmissable to anyone passing through the town at any time of year and, especially since a million-dollar-plus expansion was completed, boasts one of the most spectacular cellar door bars and restaurants in Australia. In the early days, however, the beers didn't always match the experience, with quality variable.

Since home-brewing boffin John Seltin was given his big break there in 2011, variability has become a thing of the past, with a vastly improved core range and a series of limited release specialties, such as the MIA IPA and Stubborn Russian, capturing the attention of the beer geeks. But while the venue, brewer and beers have evolved dramatically over the years, one has sat stoically amid the transformation, wondering what all the fuss is about. Even in the early days, the Staircase Porter was the brewery's old reliable and remains so today: the Rudyard Kipling's *If* of Bright's beers.

Brewer's food match
Barbecued and smoked meat dishes, dark chocolate

Availability
Year round

Where to find it
Specialist bottle shops in Victoria

Brewery and cellar door location
121 Great Alpine Road, Bright, Victoria

Brewery website
www.brightbrewery.com.au

Brown Ale

BROOKES BEER

 Ale 5.2% 6-8°C  Nonic pint glass

TASTING NOTES There's a touch of subtle Old World hops here, but essentially this smooth, dark-brown affair is all about the malt, particularly those of the chocolate and mocha variety.

THE STORY For years a craft beer wasteland, Bendigo has in recent times become something of a regional hub for better beer. Firstly, inspired by the beers they were drinking at the oasis that is the city's Dispensary Enoteca, a pair of passionate beer lovers formed Bendigo Beer and set about persuading local publicans to broaden their range, starting a ripple that turned into something of a tidal wave.

Then, in 2013, Doug Brookes and his partner, Melissa, decided to up sticks from Melbourne and turn a former abattoir into Brookes Brewery. For Doug, it was a decision that indulged his love of brewing but also offered an escape from the corporate world. For the discerning drinkers of Bendigo, it has given them a chance to drink something truly local. For everyone else, it offers another range of beers to hunt down, with this brown ale the pick of Brookes Brewery's first raft of releases.

Brewer's food match
Hearty meat dishes, roasts, smoked or barbecued meats, nut-based desserts

Availability
Year round

Where to find it
See website for full list of stockists

Brewery location
Factory 4A, Mayfair Park, 4 McDowalls Road, Bendigo East, Victoria

Brewery website
www.brookesbeer.com.au

Brown Ale

CAVALIER BREWING

 Brown ale   5.0%   8°C  Stemmed tulip glass

TASTING NOTES It's the Cavalier way to nudge the upper end stylistically; hence, a brown ale that almost tiptoes into porter territory. It's no bad thing, with caramel, chocolate and roasted notes embellished by a touch of citrusy American hops.

THE STORY The brown ale is a funny style. In many ways, it's unsexy: a corduroy pants and flat-cap combo to an IPA's afro and shimmering flares, or the Berliner-Weisse's arty black turtleneck and severe fringe. Yet it is also one that seems to instil a real passion in those who fall for its soft, multilayered malty charms. They'll tell you there are simply not enough of them around, while singing the praises of those that are in existence.

That they brewed one from day one certainly helped Cavalier win over some fans in the early days of their rapid rise from backyard brewers to joining the host of Melbourne's biggest community of nomadic brewers. That it is a bloody good take on the style, albeit one that risks nudging into porter territory, doesn't hurt either.

Brewer's food match
Slow-cooked beef cheeks or lamb's neck

Availability
Year round

Where to find it
Leading craft beer venues Australia-wide

Brewery location
Derrimut, Victoria

Brewery website
www.cavalierbeer.com.au

Hix Brown Ale
HICKINBOTHAM

 English brown **5.0%** **6-8°C**  **English pint**

TASTING NOTES This solid British-influenced brown ale from this tiny Mornington Peninsula brewery is a rich, medium-bodied brown ale that's all about the malt, displaying flavours and aromas that encompass chocolate, caramel and nuts.

THE STORY Hickinbotham of Dromana is a winery with a wonderfully idiosyncratic appeal. Run by a winemaker with an eighty-year family history in the industry, it has been hand-built using reclaimed parts of demolished banks and an old school gym. A few years ago, Hickinbotham added a tiny brewery as a side enterprise, with vineyard manager Cameron Turner bringing his home-brewing skills into play.

The brewing side of the business has since expanded significantly, helped no doubt by a gold medal for its pale ale at the 2011 Australian International Beer Awards. Like the building that houses it, the brewery itself is rather homespun, comprising former shampoo and milk vats and a mash tun on a hydraulic base that is shunted via forklift onto a metal frame outside the brewery shed, then tipped on its side to discard spent grain. The beers, particularly the brown, show what can be achieved with a little ingenuity.

Brewer's food match
Slow-cooked lamb shoulder with sour morello cherry salsa

Availability
Year round

Where to find it
All good Melbourne bottle shops

Brewery and cellar door location
194 Nepean Highway, Dromana, Victoria

Brewery website
www.hickinbotham.biz

Temptress
HOLGATE BREWHOUSE

 Chocolate porter   6.0%   6-8°C    Nonic or jar type

TASTING NOTES Dessert in a glass, this beer takes a deeply dark brown porter as its base and piles on layers of lusciousness in the form of whole vanilla beans and Dutch cocoa to create a wealth of creamy vanilla, caramel, chocolate and mocha aromas and flavours.

THE STORY It's fair to say that this beer has become an unlikely legend of the modern Australian craft beer world, and a rather unique one at that. Porters are not the most common, or indeed greatest volume-shifting of beers (drinkers seem more likely to opt for a stout, according to bar owners), yet the Temptress polls consistently highly in any popularity vote, whether among critics or the public. Brewed with both Dutch cocoa and whole vanilla beans, it would seem best suited to the colder months or as a dessert beer, yet it continues to shift units even in summer.

It proved such a winner with drinkers that it inspired a spin-off, the Empress, an imperial mocha porter that added Australian-grown coffee to the mix – and registers a full 10 per cent ABV. In turn, the Empress proved so popular that, even though it was originally brewed as a one-off for a mini beer festival, it now returns once a year for winter.

Brewer's food match
Beef and ale pie or old-fashioned self-saucing chocolate pudding

Availability
Year round

Where to find it
Many good bottle shops and restaurants Australia-wide; check website for full list of stockists

Brewery and cellar door location
79 High Street, Woodend, Victoria

Brewery website
www.holgatebrewhouse.com

Jack of Spades Porter
JAMES SQUIRE

 Brown porter **5.0%** **6-8°C**  **Broad-stemmed goblet**

TASTING NOTES The Jack of Spades is an English-style brown porter and one of the James Squire beers still brewed at the Malt Shovel Brewery where the brand was launched. It's a dark, nearly black pour with ruby tints and a creamy mouthfeel that's dominated by chocolate and a touch of roast coffee with hops very much in a support role.

THE STORY Chuck Hahn's second major Australian beer project was to head up the James Squire range from Lion's Malt Shovel Brewery. Long before craft beer really took hold, he was using the brand to push better beer drinking and the concept of beer and food pairing; today, James Squire's beers remain many drinkers' first experience of something other than a macro lager, and the brand supports beer festivals across the country. At one end of the range, the focus has been on creating more approachable (some might say dumbed-down) entry-level beers, but elsewhere you'll find prime examples of traditional ales.

The recently tweaked English IPA is a delightful, authentic treat, while this porter has always been a fine, balanced and full-flavoured take on the style.

Brewer's food match
Black forest cake, rich meat dishes, oysters

Availability
Year round

Where to find it
Australia-wide

Brewery location
99 Pyrmont Bridge Road, Camperdown, New South Wales

Brewery website
www.james-squire.com.au

Milk Porter
KOOINDA BREWERY

 Milk porter   **4.7%**   **10-12°C**  **Pint glass**

TASTING NOTES Originally a winter seasonal that has stuck around, this full-bodied beer tends to the rich and chocolatey rather than roasted realm of malts, with added sweetness from the use of lactose and only the mildest of hop influence to round things off.

THE STORY The Kooinda story is one that epitomises the very essence of small-scale brewing. A group of mates who loved beer and, in some cases, knew how to brew beer, decided to build a brewery themselves. Over a number of years, and with their own hands, they did just that, originally launching Kooinda in a tiny shed on the driveway of a suburban house, with tanks cooled by water pumped from a backyard swimming pool.

Now housed in an industrial unit where they have also installed a bar and regularly host live music, Kooinda is a brewery whose success has been built as much on their enthusiasm and roguish origins as on the popularity of punchy hop-forward beers such as their debut American Pale Ale, Hop Transfusion IPA and Black IPA (found elsewhere in this book). They can turn their hand to more old-school, malt-based British styles too, with a smooth English Red Ale and this under-discovered milk porter worth hunting down.

Availability
Year round

Brewery and cellar door location
28 Culverlands Street, Heidelberg West, Victoria

Brewery website
www.kooinda.com

Wicked Elf Porter
THE LITTLE BREWING COMPANY

 **Robust porter** **6.2%** **8°C, in winter try 12°C** **Brandy snifter**

TASTING NOTES A perfect representation of a robust porter, this nearly black beer just begs you to dive in. A rich and complex blend of chocolate and mocha on the nose, joined by flavours that add a soft back-palate bitterness, a touch of leather, subtle savoury touches and earthy, spicy English hops.

THE STORY In 2013, The Little Brewing Company added a third string to their bow. They'd already released beers under two brands, Wicked Elf and Mad Abbot, the latter home to their excellent Belgian-style ales. To this was added the first of a planned series of more 'out there' beers, called Death between the Tanks. The name refers to the theory that head brewer Warwick Little will be found in just such a spot,

given his obsessive approach to his beers and the brewing process.

It's an obsession that makes his brewery in Port Macquarie the most immaculate I have visited, complete with the most staggering array of brewing accoutrements, all arranged perfectly, of course, in rows to the side of the brew house. It's an obsession that tends to make his beers stylistically true and consistently rewarding, such as this porter, one of the more recent additions to the Wicked Elf range, which pretty much represents the style guidelines for a porter in liquid form.

Brewer's food match
Hearty winter fare

Availability
Year round

Where to find it
Good independent bottle shops, BWS, Dan Murphy's

Brewery and cellar door location
Unit 1/58 Uralla Road, Port Macquarie, New South Wales

Brewery website
www.thelittlebrewingcompany.com.au

Brown Ale
MORNINGTON PENINSULA BREWERY

 English-style brown ale   **5.0%**   **6-8°C**  **Pint glass**

TASTING NOTES A beer I never tire of, from the soft cocoa and Ovaltine aromas through its subtly complex, multilayered flavours that shift in tiny stages from caramel and toffee through to chocolate and nuts with the faintest hint of raisin. This is an Aussie classic.

THE STORY The rise of Mornington Peninsula Brewery has been one of the great success stories of the Australian craft beer revolution. While celebrating their team's success at the 2008 AFL Grand Final, mates Matt Bebe and Malcolm Maclean decided they should open a microbrewery. Two years later, pretty much to the day, they did, in an industrial unit that used to manufacture exploding golf balls just down the road from Mornington Racecourse. Soon, head brewer Andrew 'AG' Gow was winning praise around Victoria for his beers and the pattern was set.

Almost every release has been acclaimed and, despite constantly expanding, they have struggled to meet demand. Along the way a number of their beers have become, in their own way, Australian craft icons. Perhaps the most unlikely of those is their brown ale, a somewhat unfashionable style they brew so well that its fans (me included) can come across as ardent, borderline David Koresh–style proselytisers.

Brewer's food match
Anything braised or roasted; sticky date pudding

Availability
Year round

Where to find it
Good bottle shops and bars in Queensland and Victoria

Brewery and cellar door location
72 Watt Road, Mornington, Victoria

Brewery website
www.mpbrew.com.au

Porter

MORNINGTON PENINSULA BREWERY

 English-style porter   **6.0%**  **6-8°C**   **Porter**

TASTING NOTES Another fine dark beer from Mornington Peninsula, this porter goes fairly gentle on the nose, where you'll find chocolate and toffee. Things step up a notch or two on the palate where earthy hops underpin chocolate and double-shot espresso flavours, with some burnt nuts and a leathery touch creeping in late in the day.

THE STORY Since first opening their doors in October 2010, Mornington Peninsula Brewery has produced such a vast array of different beers it's pretty much impossible to say what a typical Mornington beer is, or even to describe a particular house characteristic. There have been various wheat beers, black, white, amber and imperial IPAs, English, Scotch and Irish ales, farmhouse ales … you name it,

chances are they have brewed and released it.

If there is a common thread that binds them, however, it is their approach: taking a style, then looking to squeeze every last drop of character from it. That's certainly true of their rich and fulsome porter. Originally conceived by the head brewer as a 'Premiership Porter' in anticipation of his beloved St Kilda playing in the 2010 AFL Grand Final, it is, thankfully, rather more of a triumph than the Saints were that day.

Brewer's food match
Dark chocolate; cheese (blue Roquefort)

Availability
Seasonal (cooler months)

Where to find it
Good bottle shops and bars in
Queensland and Victoria

Brewery and cellar door location
72 Watt Road, Mornington, Victoria

Brewery website
www.mpbrew.com.au

Angry Man Brown Ale
MURRAY'S CRAFT BREWING

 American brown ale 6.5%  6-12°C US-style shaker pint

TASTING NOTES This is a brown ale that takes the American approach to the style, celebrating both malt (of the nutty, caramel and toasted variety) and hops (of the pungent, olfactory-bothering New World variety) with a vengeance.

THE STORY It can be harder to keep track of beers from Murray's, a prolific New South Wales brewery, than most. Not only do they release a kaleidoscopic array of beers each year, made up of a core range embellished by returning seasonals and even more limited one-offs, but their branding is equal parts inspired, colourful and schizophrenic.

What's more, they're not afraid to change the name of their beers either. Ever since deciding to change the name of their pale ale from Nirvana to Angry Man Pale Ale, there's been an extra trap laid for the easily befuddled. The original Murray's beer to bear the Angry Man moniker is this brown ale, which is the equivalent of pushing heaps of pumped-up malt and a ton of punchy hops into a caged ring and inviting them to battle it out to the death, only to have to declare a draw fifteen epic rounds later.

Brewer's food match
Rib eye steak, smoked lamb shoulder

Availability
Seasonal

Where to find it
On draught Australia-wide at good craft beer venues; bottled seasonally

and available Australia-wide at good independent bottle shops and online

Brewery and cellar door location
3443 Nelson Bay Road, Bobs Farm, New South Wales

Brewery website
www.murraysbrewingco.com.au

Tailpipe Big Ass Brown Ale
PRICKLY MOSES BREWERY

 **American brown ale** **7.1%** **8-10°C** **Spiegelau IPA glass or pint glass**

TASTING NOTES Big ass, hey? So what does that translate to? A sizeable booze content, but one that's well hidden by the equally sizeable servings of chocolate, caramel and roasted malts and firm hop bitterness that give way to a lingering sweetness on the palate.

THE STORY Prickly Moses is one of the stalwarts of the Victorian microbrewing industry, itself the largest of any state in Australia. Sharing its home with a winery on the edge of the Otway Ranges, it has steadily embellished the 'playing it safe' core range it launched with. There have been annual releases inspired by French and Belgian farmhouse styles, beers created with wild hops harvested from nearby fields, beers brewed with locally harvested fruit and beers that re-create historical recipes.

At one point, during a period when the man who has gone on to form BrewCult was part of the brewing team, there was also a flirtation with bigger, heavily hopped American styles. Of those, the pick was this Big Ass Brown Ale, a beer in which they ramped up the grain bill and the hop dosage in equal measure. Like the classic American car on its label, it's brash rather than elegant, but surely that's the point.

Brewer's food match
Rich red or game meat; rich desserts such as chocolate mud cake

Availability
Seasonal (August–September) until sold out

Where to find it
Many good independent bottle shops such as Purvis Beer; see website for stockists

Brewery and cellar door location
10 Hoveys Road, Barongarook, Victoria

Brewery website
www.pricklymoses.com.au

Blacksmiths Porter
TOOBORAC BREWERY

 Porter 5.5% 8-10°C Mug

TASTING NOTES Tooborac's best beer presents almost opaque in the glass: black with a tan head that leaves lacing as it's consumed. Aromas are dominated by dark chocolate, cocoa and mocha, with flavours of roast coffee, dark fruit, burned treacle and licorice leading into a long, lingering and roasty finish.

THE STORY Since taking over a beautiful old bluestone hotel on the Northern Highway approximately 100 kilometres north of Melbourne, James and Val Carlin have created a lovely rural restaurant and brewery setup. The beers from the brewery, which is located in a cute former Cobb & Co stable at the rear, have steadily improved since their first ale hit the hotel taps in 2009, and today taste as good as they ever have.

This porter is the pick of the bunch, a bunch that has been appearing with greater frequency across Victoria's beer venues in recent times. It could have something to do with the Tooborac 'Beerbulance', a converted ambulance into the side of which they have installed draught taps, giving them a highly convenient – and rather eye-catching – way of refreshing the crowds at beer events.

Brewer's food match
Irish stew, chilli pizza, chocolate pudding

Availability
Year round

Where to find it
Selected venues around Victoria; see website for stockists

Brewery and cellar door location
5115 Northern Hwy, Tooborac, Victoria

Brewery website
www.tooborachotel.com.au

Dark Ale
WHITE RABBIT

 Open fermented dark ale **4.9%** **4.8-5°C**  **Tulip glass**

TASTING NOTES Despite its name, it pours a light brown and possesses the sweet, nutty and fruity aromas of an English ale. Flavours are initially led by chocolate and caramel with some fruitiness that comes through later, adding complexity. Perhaps not hitting the heights of its earlier, darker, roastier days, but a clean, balanced and approachable dark ale nonetheless.

THE STORY The first beer from Little Creatures' brother brewery in Healesville in the Yarra Valley is brewed in one of Australia's only breweries to feature open fermenters. It's also one of the bestselling dark beers in the country. On the face of things, alongside White Rabbit's White Ale, it appears to be one half of the most streamlined range of beers from any brewery in the country.

Head to the cellar door and you'll find a quite different situation, however. The brewing team always has a number of tiny experiments going on alongside their stainless steel tanks, often featuring wooden barrels and wild yeasts. There is rarely more than a keg or two of each, and you'll never find them outside the cellar door, the Little Creatures Dining Hall in Fitzroy, or at special events, but they are always worth sampling on the rare occasions they do appear.

Availability
Year round

Where to find it
Available at all good bottle shops
Australia-wide

Brewery and cellar door location
316 Maroondah Highway, Healesville, Victoria

Brewery website
www.whiterabbitbeer.com.au

STOUTS
AND
IMPERIAL
STOUTS

Stouts and Imperial Stouts

Stouts are the darkest of all beers, typically ranging in colour from a dark brown through to the deepest jet black, and are often opaque. Imperial stouts are, as the name suggests, bigger and bolder versions of these beers: higher in alcohol, thicker in body, more complex in aroma and flavour, and sharing some characteristics with fortified wines.

It is a style that developed from English porters. Originally the term 'stout' was used in England to describe a stronger version of any style of beer, but by the late nineteenth century it was most commonly used in conjunction with strong porters, with the phrase 'stout porter' ultimately shortened to simply 'stout', leaving two beer styles with much in common to go their own ways.

As well as being typically stronger, stouts were generally roastier and more bitter, with the use of roasted barley lending the style the distinct characteristics it shares with roast coffee, as well as a bitterness derived from the malt in addition to that derived from hops.

Over time, stout itself diverged into many variants. Among them are the dry Irish stout style made most famous by Guinness, milk or sweet stouts that feature the use of lactose to add a creamy sweetness to the finished beer, and oatmeal stouts in which the addition of oats gives a fullness and softness to the mouthfeel.

Stouts also have a proud heritage in Australia. While they are not obviously suited to the country's hot climate, there are many brands with a long, unbroken stout lineage that survived the rationalisation and homogenisation of the beer industry during the twentieth century. In many ways, they are anomalies, but welcome anomalies for that. Beers such as Southwark Old Stout or CUB's Sheaf Stout really had no right to survive the transformation of Australia's beer culture as a handful of dominant industrial brewers turned us into a nation of lager swillers. But they did.

Their endurance is mirrored across the former British Empire. Various export stouts were transported to the colonies, some proving so popular that many were licensed to be brewed by local brewers on the ground. To this day, you can find variants of Guinness Foreign Extra Stout across the globe as well as other beers, such as the fine Lion Stout produced by the Lion Brewery of Sri Lanka, which was founded in late–nineteenth century colonial times.

Pleasingly, you can peruse the shelves of bottle shops today and see Southwark Old Stout still bearing its deeply unfashionable livery like a relic from another era. Even more pleasingly, it tastes great and costs very little, making it, like Coopers' excellent Best Extra Stout, one of the best-value beers in the country.

Today, Australia is home to a remarkably large number of quality stouts. When compiling this list of beers, I was surprised at how many made the final cut. In many cases, when selecting the best beer from many of the smaller and younger breweries, it was their stout that stood out.

The list also highlights just what a versatile style this can be. There are locally brewed sweet and dry stouts, one that features both lactose and Madagascan vanilla and others brewed with oatmeal. Some have been brewed to the same recipe for generations; a couple come from breweries that are barely a year old.

Recently, the explosive growth of craft beer both globally and in Australia has seen a rise in the popularity of many extreme beer styles, among them the imperial stout. Originally an export-strength 'stout porter' brewed in England to be sent to the Baltic states and Russia in the 1800s, it is significantly higher in alcohol than normal stouts, often around 10 per cent ABV. Rich, fulsome, hearty and warming, these beers are palate-engulfing delights awash with chocolate, coffee, molasses, treacle, vanilla, dark fruits and much more besides, often with vinous qualities, too.

Each winter seems to bring forth more from Australian brewers, frequently of an astoundingly high standard. Some are barrel aged; some feature Belgian yeasts that add another layer of quirky complexity. They seem to keep getting bigger too. One of the first to be released annually was from Red Hill Brewery on the Mornington Peninsula;

it remains an excellent, multi-layered beer but, at 8.1 percent, now sits alongside many that tower over it in terms of size and impact. Often these beasts of the imperial stout world are released in rather decadent 750 ml champagne-style bottles, in keeping with their suitability for sharing amongst friends. Ideally with a large chunk of quality blue cheese.

TOP OF THE HOPS

My top three stouts:

MOO BREW STOUT

THIRSTY CROW VANILLA MILK STOUT

COOPERS BREWERY BEST EXTRA STOUT

My top three imperial stouts:

NAIL BREWING CLOUT STOUT

MORNINGTON PENINSULA BREWERY RUSSIAN IMPERIAL STOUT

FERAL BREWING BORIS RUSSIAN IMPERIAL STOUT

Stout

4 PINES BREWING COMPANY

 Dry Irish stout **5.1%** **6-8°C** **Pint**

TASTING NOTES Although pitched as a dry Irish stout, this delicious, nigh-on-black beer with a surprisingly fulsome body for just 5.1 per cent ABV, sits right in the middle of the stout flavour range. Expect everything from creamy caramel to hints of espresso, with raisins, chocolate and nuts along the way.

THE STORY They love their hijinks at 4 Pines. The mix of surfers and fresh-faced beer lovers that make up the owners and staff at the brewery are only too eager to throw a party, don fancy dress, or accidentally draw the ire of members of a world religion through their colourful marketing (true story). Their approach to marketing is less 'the sky's the limit' than 'the sky is no limit', as evidenced by their ongoing attempts, alongside the Vostock Space Agency, to turn 4 Pines Stout into the world's first 'space beer'.

The last footage they released featured a couple of people appearing to try and drink the beer from plastic bottles on a sub-orbital weightlessness training flight. Just how close this places the Stout to becoming a regular tipple on the International Space Station is open to question. What is certain is that the Stout – a former trophy winner at the Australian International Beer Awards – is a beautifully balanced beer from the Manly-based brewery.

Brewer's food match
Dessert beer; match with rich or light flavours, chocolate or ice cream

Availability
Year round

Where to find it
National retailers, good independents and on tap at selected venues

Brewery location
4F, 9–13 Winbourne Road, Brookvale, New South Wales

Cellar door
29/43-45 E Esplanade, Manly, New South Wales

Brewery website
www.4pinesbeer.com.au

Mussel Stout

BELLARINE BREWING COMPANY

 Stout 5.2% 8-10°C  Snifter or balloon

TASTING NOTES The fresh Portarlington blue mussels added to the brew the day they're pulled from the sea add a drying, salty brininess to this stout, a nice counterpoint to the dark chocolate, licorice and coffee flavours of the base beer.

THE STORY In 2013, there was a spate of beers released in Australia featuring seafood, mussels in particular (including one conceived by the author of this book, which also included oysters in the mix). It was probably a never-to-be-repeated coincidence, with mussel stouts being a particularly rare style with its origins in the UK.

That said, such a beer has been the calling card for a small Victorian brewery found on the Bellarine Peninsula for a number of years now. Head brewer Tim Page-Walker created the beer as a one-off for the annual Portarlington Mussel Festival but, such was its popularity, it remains to this day. The brewery, which shares a site with Bellarine Estate Winery, likes to take local landmarks as inspiration for its beers – Lonsdale Lager, Queenscliff Ale, for example – but none has had the success of the bivalves from just down the road.

Brewer's food match
Hearty and rich meals; stews, steaks, surf and turf

Availability
Year round

Where to find it
Finer beer merchants, bottle shops, restaurants and licensed cafes in Melbourne, Geelong, Ballarat, the Bellarine and the Surf Coast; online at website

Brewery and cellar door location
2270 Portarlington Road, Bellarine, Victoria

Brewery website
www.bellarinebrewingcompany.com.au

Ramjet Imperial Stout

BOATROCKER BREWERY

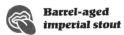 **Barrel-aged imperial stout** **10.2%**  **12-18°C** **Snifter**

TASTING NOTES Having spent several months in whisky barrels from New World Distillery, this limited release from Boatrocker has big vanilla and soft oak tones, as well as a touch of whisky, which embellish the cocoa powder and rummy, dark fruits of the base beer to create an almost liqueur-like chocolatey treat.

THE STORY Prior to taking ownership of his brewery, Boatrocker founder Matt Houghton always professed a fascination with many of the world's more adventurous styles. This was despite the fact that the beers he was having brewed under contract tended to play things safe: an American-style pale and a pilsner, for example. But as soon as the ink on the paperwork for the Braeside brewery site was dry, he set about indulging that fascination.

Dozens of wine barrels were purchased for a sour beer program, while a series of varied Belgian beers soon appeared.

The beer that turned most heads in the early days, however, was the Ramjet, a whisky barrel–aged imperial stout tipping the scales above 10 per cent yet drinking a little like a smooth, creamy liqueur coffee. Given it was one of the very first beers put through the secondhand brewery he had picked up from Tasmania not long before, it bodes well for Boatrocker's future within the Australian beer world.

Brewer's food match
Gorgonzola dulce or a young Stilton

Availability
Seasonal

Where to find it
Good craft bottle shops

Brewery and cellar door location
51 Macbeth Street, Braeside, Victoria

Brewery website
www.boatrocker.com.au

Stout

CASCADE BREWERY

 Stout **5.8%** **10-12°C**  **Footed beer glass**

TASTING NOTES More deep brown than black, this stout combines aromas you'd expect, such as high-percentage cocoa dark chocolate and nuttiness, with some that are less expected, such as a touch of iodine and seaweed. As it warms, soft caramel flavours come into play, ending with a gentle roasted bitterness that lingers long.

THE STORY A couple of years back, I was invited to Hobart to join Cascade's maltster on a tour of the barley fields and Cascade's in-house maltings prior to the annual brew of their First Harvest with the then long-standing head brewer Max Burslem. We sampled most of their range, including new additions that have since bitten the dust, with brewery representatives extolling each one's

virtue. But when we hit the pubs of Hobart later that evening, Max was soon onto his brewery's stout. As were the rest of us.

In the world of mainstream lagers, Cascade's are better than most in Australia; their standout beer, however, is this one. For a long time, you had to travel to Tasmania to find it; thankfully, following a full rebranding at Cascade in 2013, one that highlights its heritage and the beautiful old brewery in the foothills of Mount Wellington, the beer has made its way onto the mainland, too.

Brewer's food match
Chocolate pudding with cream

Availability
Year round

Where to find it
Dan Murphy's and selected bottle shops
Australia-wide

Brewery and cellar door location
140 Cascade Road, South Hobart, Tasmania

Brewery website
www.cascadebreweryco.com.au

King Kong Stout

CLARE VALLEY BREWING COMPANY

 Extra stout   6.0%   8-12°C  Pint or tulip glass

TASTING NOTES This early release from the Clare Valley Brewing Company is a distinctly dark, full-bodied affair with a creamy mouthfeel and excellent carbonation. It sits at the deeper, darker end of the stout scale, with roasted barley, dark chocolate and coffee aromas and burnt treacle and plums to taste as well.

THE STORY It's not uncommon for winemakers to become brewers. Or, indeed, for wineries to release a beer or two. In the latter case, what tends to happen is they ask someone to make beer for them (with variable input into recipe development from the winery) then slap their own name and label on the bottle.

The owners of Jeanneret Wines in Clare Valley took a far harder route: they bought an old brewery (one that required rather more work to get operational than they'd hoped) and installed it at their winery. Under the guidance of South Australian brewing guru Stephen Nelsen, they launched with a range of ales and a grape cider in 2013, and this rich and luscious stout is the pick of the bunch. The full range is available at the cellar door in Auburn, and there are plans to brew beers from entirely estate-grown-and-harvested ingredients in years to come.

Brewer's food match
Steak, hearty stews, or a rich, creamy chocolate dessert

Availability
Year round

Where to find it
Throughout South Australia

Brewery location
1 Jeanneret Road, Sevenhill, South Australia

Cellar door
20 Main North Road, Auburn, South Australia

Brewery website
www.clarevalleybrewing.com.au

Best Extra Stout
COOPERS BREWERY

 Stout   6.3%   10°C  **Coopers pint glass (roll bottle before serving)**

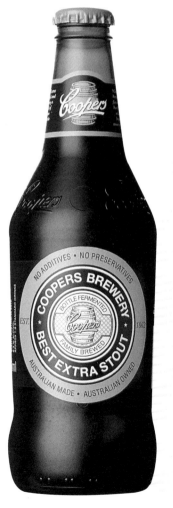

TASTING NOTES An Aussie classic that ages gracefully, this beer is deeply dark with a tan head, a blast from the past that is a beautifully deep and complex melange of aromas and flavours that, depending on age, can encompass milk chocolate, roast coffee, tobacco, dark fruits, molasses and dark cocoa.

THE STORY Coopers Best Extra Stout is like the Old Faithful of the Australian beer world. It is reliably, consistently excellent – an old-fashioned, reasonably full-bodied stout with complexity and depth that never lets you down. It's a reliable fallback for the beer lover who finds themselves on a tight budget, and is always there when you need it; thanks to Coopers' success in spreading their core beers into pretty much every corner of the country, chances are that even in a sports bar in northern Queensland, a bottle shop in country SA or an outback shack in the middle of nowhere, there will be a bottle with a yellow label ready to rescue your palate from macro-lager mediocrity. Better still, it's probably been sat there for years, meaning it's got the benefits of age on its side.

Brewer's food match
Oysters, pork, beef, soft or hard cheeses, all desserts

Availability
Year round, especially well suited to winter months

Where to find it
Most leading retailers and selected venues

Brewery and cellar door location
461 South Road, Regency Park, South Australia

Brewery website
www.coopers.com.au

Boris Russian Imperial Stout
FERAL BREWING

 Imperial stout   **10.1%**   **10°C** *Nonic pint*

TASTING NOTES Here is another imperial stout that belies its size due to the remarkably smooth way it goes down. That said, don't confuse its approachability with simplicity; this velvety trophy winner offers up everything from tar and molasses to coffee and roasted nuts, spicy hops and treacle to chocolate and toffee.

THE STORY Not only does Feral Brewing create one of the most colourful (and very possibly the finest) ranges of beer anywhere in Australia, but its head brewer knows how to win medals, too. That may seem a daft thing to say when results speak for themselves: no Aussie brewer has won more trophies over the decade since the Swan Valley brewery opened its doors. But Brendan Varis has shown that knowing your beer inside out, as well as brewing a damn fine one, helps weigh down the shelves of any trophy cabinet.

The Hop Hog IPA has regularly cleaned up in the American pale ale, not IPA, category, while in 2013, another of their much-loved and much-heralded beers, Boris, took out best porter despite being labeled an imperial stout. Unsurprisingly in a world in which the most ardent beer geeks take pride in shouting the loudest and poking with the sharpest of (Twitter-shaped) sticks, there were a few grumbles. The easiest way to ignore them is to pour a glass of Boris and let it conduct its virtual full-body massage on you via your tastebuds.

Brewer's food match
Flourless chocolate cake

Availability
Year round

Where to find it
Specialist beer bars

Brewery and cellar door location
152 Haddrill Road, Baskerville, Western Australia

Brewery website
www.feralbrewing.com.au

Hatlifter Stout

GRAND RIDGE BREWERY

 Australian stout   **4.9%**  **4-6°C**   **Traditional Irish stout goblet**

TASTING NOTES This old-school beer from the brewery with some of the most old-school labels in the land offers up some initial sweetness. But soon it gives in to the dark side, as bitter cocoa and espresso-like flavours take over, leading to a lingering, roast-dry finish.

THE STORY Grand Ridge owner Eric Walters is one of the Australian beer industry's most passionate and loquacious advocates, particularly when it comes to his own beers (and the steaks carved from the cattle he rears on spent grain from said beers, to be served up at the brewery restaurant). The brewery's hometown is Mirboo North, in East Gippsland; Mirboo means 'magic water', which Eric will tell you leads to magic beer.

It's a magic best experienced at the darker end of the Grand Ridge range, where the Moonshine (featured elsewhere in this book), Supershine, Mirboo Midnight and this sweet stout exist. Like the brewery's branding, the Hatlifter is an old-school affair, based on the Irish stout style but sweeter and creamier than most, and one that is standing the test of time admirably.

Brewer's food match
High-quality Belgian dark chocolate, mud cake

Availability
Year round

Where to find it
Brewery Direct, Dan Murphy's, First Choice and all good independent bottle shops

Brewery and cellar door location
1 Baromi Road, Mirboo, North Victoria

Brewery website
www.grand-ridge.com.au

RIS

HARGREAVES HILL

 Russian imperial stout **10.0-12.0%**  **8-10°C** **Brandy snifter**

TASTING NOTES If there are gateway beers for newcomers to craft beer, what are beers like this: doors to the inner sanctum? A truly huge beer, and truly rewarding too, this annual release holds nothing back, unleashing wave after thunderous wave of heavy roasted espresso, licorice, brown sugar, caramel, vanilla and chocolate liqueur in a luxuriant, engine oil–like body.

THE STORY Even in the darkest days of the Australian beer industry, when Coopers was pretty much the only shining light amid the gloom (and struggling itself), you could still find a number of decent locally brewed stouts if you looked hard enough. These days, with the craft beer revolution having taken hold, it has reached the point where the number of imperial stouts rises every winter. And, while it is true that the more you throw into a beer, the easier it is to hide faults, it is also true that many of these local beasts are genuinely fantastic brews, as evidenced by the number of gold medals and trophies handed out to them at the Australian International Beer Awards.

Hargreaves Hill's RIS has picked up one of those gold medals and, like the brewery's Phoenix, is a rarely brewed limited release. And, also like the Phoenix, it is a rather opulent masterpiece that tips the scales well in excess of 10 per cent and warrants sipping and savouring over a long, slow evening, preferably in the company of like-minded mates.

Brewer's food match
Good selection of cheeses

Availability
Annual – limited release of bottles and kegs

Where to find it
Selected bottle shops and venues

Brewery location
60/64–86 Beresford Road, Lilydale, Victoria

Cellar door
25 Bell Street, Yarra Glen, Victoria

Brewery website
www.hargreaveshill.com.au

Stout

HARGREAVES HILL

 Foreign export stout **6.2%** **8-10°C** **Nonic glass**

TASTING NOTES Although the ABV has been toned down from its initial 6.7 per cent, this stout remains a beer of depth. Floral hop, fresh-roasted coffee bean and salty aromas lead off before the no-holds-barred malt assault on the palate begins, taking the form of cocoa, dark fruits, molasses and a lingering roasty, woody bitterness.

THE STORY Certain breweries can be said to have something of a house style. It may not feature in all of their beers, but will be a running thread through many of them. Feral has a signature US hop combo, Murray's uses nothing but Kiwi hops, Bridge Road loves to experiment with new Australian varieties, and so on.

Hargreaves Hill without doubt takes a traditionalist's approach to the styles it favours, but it also possesses an uncanny ability to obtain a lovely, soft, almost pillow-like malt character on the mid-palate with many of its beers. It's as if, midway through each mouthful, the beer tucks in your tongue for the night and presents it with a mug of Milo, heated just right. It's present in this stout, with that comforting mug of Milo accompanied by a broad range of malt flavours in a beer that deserves a far broader audience than it currently enjoys.

Brewer's food match
Pâté

Availability
Year round

Where to find it
Good craft beer bottle shops and venues

Brewery location
60/64–86 Beresford Road, Lilydale, Victoria

Cellar door
25 Bell Street, Yarra Glen, Victoria

Brewery website
www.hargreaveshill.com.au

Chocolate Oatmeal Stout

LOBETHAL BIERHAUS

 Sweet stout **5.8%** **Slightly chilled** **Brandy balloon**

TASTING NOTES This is a smooth, sweet stout that gains a softness on the palate from the use of oatmeal. Sweet chocolate aromas are joined by coffee and vanilla on the palate, finishing with a soft roasted bitterness.

THE STORY In 2013, vintage motor racing enthusiast and banker-turned-brewer Alistair Turnbull spent a cool $500,000 expanding and upgrading his brewery in a converted tweed factory, growing from three to thirteen tanks and installing new equipment to give him greater consistency and control over his fine range of lagers and ales.

Whether that means anyone outside South Australia is any more likely to get their hands on his beers is debatable. Demand within his home state means any bar owner keen to tap one interstate needs to be darned persistent to get it across the border. It's no bad thing, as a visit to the brewery bar and restaurant, where you can sample up to fourteen different Lobethal beers on tap at any one time – ideally accompanied by a mound of spicy chicken wings – is a trip well worth making. This Chocolate Oatmeal Stout really comes into its own on tap, too.

Brewer's food match
Chocolate dessert, flavoursome cheese

Availability
Year round

Where to find it
Throughout South Australia
in independent bottle shops,
restaurants and hotels

Brewery and cellar door location
3A Main Street, Lobethal,
South Australia

Brewery website
www.bierhaus.com.au

Choc Hops
MILDURA BREWERY

 **Chocolate stout** **5.0%**  **8-10°C** **Balloon**

TASTING NOTES An after-dinner chocolate in a glass. This dark brown beer with ruby hints and a crema head is so luscious and opulent it's hard to believe it's only 5 per cent alcohol. Each mouthful is awash with vanilla, fudge and smooth Belgian milk chocolate. Thankfully, there's enough drying bitterness to lend it a little balance.

THE STORY People knew what to expect from Mildura. For years they had been producing a range of consistently safe and approachable lagers and ales from their home in the iconic Astor Theatre.

Then they rocked up to a microbrewery showcase in Melbourne's Federation Square in 2009 and started pouring samples of a beer called Choc Hops. This sumptuous explosion of all things chocolate was inspired by head brewer Rod Williams's favourite brew from his home country, Youngs Double Chocolate Stout, and is a fine tribute. It showed what Mildura's brewers were capable of with the handbrake loosened, although it was some time before they were genuinely freewheeling.

In 2013, owner Stefano de Pieri invested in some smaller tanks and encouraged Rod and his team to start playing around. The result means that Choc Hops, which remains a popular annual release, now counts everything from Belgian-inspired sour fruit beers to dense, English old ales and floral farmhouse ales as stablemates.

Brewer's food match
Smoky barbecued pork ribs, tiramisu made using Choc Hops instead of marsala and coffee

Availability
Seasonal (autumn/Easter)

Where to find it
On tap and in bottle at selected bars and bottle shops. See website for full list of stockists.

Brewery and cellar door location
20 Langtree Avenue, Mildura, Victoria

Brewery website
www.mildurabrewery.com.au

Stout

MOO BREW

 Stout **7.9%** **10-12°C**  **Large red wine glass**

TASTING NOTES The straight Seasonal Stout is an oily black beast with a dark tan head that's all about the dark side: chocolate, espresso, licorice and a firm, lingering bitterness. The barrel-aged version tends to include vanilla, oak and soft, sweet caramel, sometimes a sharp acidity, too.

THE STORY Of all their beautifully presented, art-adorned beers, the most spoken about and hotly anticipated Moo Brew release is undoubtedly their stout, which used to come in two parts. For a few years up until 2013, the beer – an 8 per cent ABV, smothering abyss of dark malts and lingering bitterness – would be released in draught-only form between autumn and winter. A portion would be kept back to be aged in oak,

then bottled almost a year later for release in a number of seriously limited 330 ml bottles with a 'Vintage' tag and a $25 per stubby price to match.

From 2014 on, the vintage release will be no more, with two versions of the Stout – one of which will spend some time in barrels, although not the nine months prior vintages did – both released concurrently around the country. In any form, it was one of the first big stouts released by a contemporary Australian microbrewery and remains one of the best.

Brewer's food match
Dark chocolate–based desserts

Availability
Year round

Where to find it
Australia-wide

Brewery location
76A Cove Hill Road, Bridgewater, Tasmania

Cellar door
Museum of Old and New Art (MONA), 655 Main Road, Berriedale, Tasmania

Brewery website
www.moobrew.com.au

Russian Imperial Stout

MORNINGTON PENINSULA BREWERY

 **Russian imperial stout**   **9.5%**    **8-10°C**   **Goblet, balloon**

TASTING NOTES Rapidly becoming an Aussie classic, this oily beast pours a jet black with a thick mocha head and manages to be a no-holds-barred yet approachable imperial stout. There's wonderful balance between the sweeter chocolate and alcohol characters and the bitter roasted ones, with plenty of hops to keep the mountain of dark malts in check without distracting from them.

THE STORY Over the years, Mornington Peninsula Brewery has released a number of imperial beers – in other words, high-octane, high-ABV versions of more 'standard' beers. The first to capture the attention of the local beer cognoscenti was their imperial IPA. An imperial amber followed too, but it is their Russian imperial stout that has become perhaps the brewery's defining beer.

Awed whispers began surrounding the beer as soon as the first batch was released in 2012. The following May, during Melbourne's Good Beer Week, a bar owner who knows a thing or two about beer told me he had just tapped a keg he'd been cellaring for 12 months specially for the festival. It was, he declared, without a doubt the best Victorian beer he'd ever served at his bar. Less than 24 hours later, the brewery owners made their way home from the Australian International Beer Awards with the trophy for Best Stout tucked deservedly under their arm.

Brewer's food match
Anything rich and decadent

Availability
Seasonal

Where to find it
Good bottle shops and bars in Queensland and Victoria

Brewery and cellar door location
72 Watt Road, Mornington, Victoria

Brewery website
www.mpbrew.com.au

Surefoot Stout

MOUNTAIN GOAT

 Stout **4.9%** **5°C** **Handled pint mug**

TASTING NOTES This is an Aussie craft beer stalwart and former trophy winner that sits nicely in the middle of the stout category: a little bit sweet and a little bit dry, but not too much of either. Barely changed from its earliest days (because it didn't have to), it's a beautifully balanced blend of sweet chocolate and butter roasted malts with a smidgeon of coffee.

THE STORY When weighing up their entry into the brewing industry back in the mid- to late-90s, friends Dave Bonighton and Cam Hines discussed launching with this beer; apparently, they even considered becoming a stout and dark beer–only brewery. In the end, the Hightail Ale came first, but when the Surefoot Stout followed it wasted little time in becoming a much-loved winter tipple.

Like the Hightail, it has in some ways been superseded by bigger, bolshier takes on the stout style since – Mountain Goat even brews a Bigfoot version on the rare occasion their increasingly busy brewing schedule allows. But, now released in an annual 'Rare Breed' capacity, this sweet stout remains what it always has been: smooth, bittersweet, balanced and begging you to come back for more. It's a less hairy goat than it may once have seemed, for sure, but is welcomed with open arms by its legion of fans each and every Melbourne winter.

Brewer's food match
Steak and kidney pie, blue cheese

Availability
Seasonal (winter)

Where to find it
Beer geek stores Australia-wide

Brewery and cellar door location
80 North Street, Richmond, Victoria

Brewery website
www.goatbeer.com.au

Heart of Darkness
MURRAY'S CRAFT BREWING

 Belgian imperial stout  9.6% 8-12°C Chalice

TASTING NOTES The use of a Belgian Trappist yeast adds an appealingly quirky twist to this, one of many imperial stouts released by Murray's over the years. Its effect is to round out the mouthfeel of the beer and also to add subtle, fruity esters, intrigue and port-like qualities to the more typical dark malt characters of an imperial stout.

THE STORY There will be many passionate beer lovers who will claim it is sacrilege that Murray's Wild Thing is not in this book. Along with the Heart of Darkness, it is one of two imperial stouts released by the Port Stephens brewery every winter. And, while the Wild Thing's epic collision of an immovable object (a mountain of dark, foreboding malts) with an unstoppable force (a small forest of Kiwi hops) makes for a beer that is nothing short of marvellous, it is the Heart of Darkness that makes these pages.

Taking its name from Conrad's dark novella, Heart of Darkness has a rather twisted nature of its own. Head brewer Shawn Sherlock used a Belgian Trappist yeast to give the beer its unique and intriguing character. In the past the brewery has released an oak-aged version too, with the time in barrels adding some mellowing vanilla and caramel characteristics; hopefully, Murray's can be enticed to carry out the experiment again.

Brewer's food match
Roquefort blue cheese

Availability
Seasonal (winter)

Where to find it
Available online and at good craft beer venues Australia-wide

Brewery and cellar door location
3443 Nelson Bay Road, Bobs Farm, New South Wales

Brewery website
www.murraysbrewingco.com.au

Clout Stout

NAIL BREWING

 Russian imperial stout 10.7% 15°C  Essence

TASTING NOTES Each year's vintage has seen Clout get bigger, like a bottled Hulk working itself into a rage. And each year it has been awesome, in the original meaning of the word. A jet-black, viscous beauty that crawls down the glass and coats the gullet, it's everything you could want in a traditional Russian imperial stout, with flavours from rich chocolate and molasses to coffee and vanilla with a big earthy bitterness holding it all together.

THE STORY It takes a fair amount of chutzpah to charge $70 for a bottle of beer. But just try and find somebody who has handed over $70 for a bottle of Nail Brewing's Clout Stout that has a bad word to say about it, or wants a refund. Originally released in 2010 and annually since

in a limited number of individually numbered and boxed 750 ml bottles, it is becoming something of a dynasty in the Australian craft beer world: an event beer.

Each release has been slightly different from the previous, but all are beers brewed in the traditional Russian imperial stout style, and held at the brewery for months on end by the brewer until he believes they are in peak condition for release. That said, they are beers that improve with age too, developing further nuances in what are already fantastically complex and rewarding beers even in their relative youth. You just have to have the willpower to resist…

Brewer's food match
Best drunk with someone special

Availability
Seasonal

Where to find it
Available Australia-wide

Brewery location
Bassendean, Western Australia

Brewery website
www.nailbrewing.com.au

Stout

NAIL BREWING

 **Oatmeal stout** **6.0%**  **8°C** **Tulip glass**

TASTING NOTES This is a beer that is as soothing as it is multilayered and complex. Rolled oats lend a smooth, full mouthfeel to this serial award winner that reveals all manner of chocolate, dark cocoa, nutty and coffee flavours as it warms, tied up with a soft, spicy hop finish.

THE STORY Nail Brewing founder John Stallwood is more than just a brewer. He helped get the Western Australian Brewing Association off the ground, founded microbrewing.com.au to provide an online resource for the Australian craft beer industry, was pivotal in launching the Perth Royal Beer Show and has assisted other brewers in his home state. He's also lucky to be alive, having been the victim of an unprovoked king hit assault in Fremantle in 2004 that left him in a coma.

Now, with his head partially constructed from titanium and having steadily eased his way back into the brewing world, he is part-owner of the impressive BrewCorp facility that he co-owns with long-term sparring partner Brendan Varis of Feral. It's allowing Nail's beers to finally start reaching the audience they should have done years ago, which means beer lovers will be able to discover for themselves just why beers such as this excellent oatmeal stout have collected gold medals and trophies like they're going out of fashion.

Brewer's food match
Chocolate

Availability
Year round

Where to find it
Available Australia-wide

Brewery location
Bassendean, Western Australia

Brewery website
www.nailbrewing.com.au

The Ox

RED DUCK BREWERY

 **Imperial stout** **9.4%** **Any**  **Your favourite**

TASTING NOTES A devilishly dark, oily beer that pours with a thin tan head, The Ox was one of the first imperial stouts to come out of the Australian craft beer industry. Recently, this annual release has had a tweak to make it slightly roastier, while you'll find licorice, chocolate, plums and a lingering bitterness in every bottle, too.

THE STORY These days, Red Duck co-owner and head brewer Scott Wilson-Browne has a well-established reputation within craft beer circles as a vaguely unhinged experimenter nonpareil. But back before he regularly knocked out twenty or more beers that had seen the insides of barrels, been brewed without hops, or with nettles, or been deliberately scorched or pilfered from the recipes of the Middle Ages, it was this beer that, more than any other, grabbed the attention of those seeking something a little out of the ordinary from a homegrown brewer.

Brewed solely from first runnings (the very first, and thus densest, of the warm, sugary wort to be drained from the mash tun) and usually brewed twice on the same day to ensure these first runnings fill a fermenter, it's something of a labour of love that usually entails a twenty-two-hour brew day. Scott likes to think of it as his stab at the legendary Dark Lord from the US's Three Floyds, a beer released on one day a year (Dark Lord Day) and only sold to people that visit the brewery in person. Thankfully, you can pick up Red Duck's The Ox rather more easily.

Brewer's food match
Braised hickory-smoked brisket or freshly shucked oysters with a squeeze of lemon

Availability
Limited

Where to find it
Good boutique bottle shops, bars and restaurants

Brewery location
Ballarat, Victoria

Cellar door
11A Michaels Drive, Alfredton, Victoria

Brewery website
www.redduckbeer.com.au

Imperial Stout
RED HILL BREWERY

 **Imperial stout** **8.0%**  **8°C** **English pint**

TASTING NOTES Australian microbrewing's longest-running annual imperial stout release has been joined by some far bigger and more boisterous peers in recent times. It still stacks up, however, with plenty of depth within its 8.1 per cent body, one that starts sweet and creamy with brown sugar, dark fruit and mocha characteristics before turning steadily more roasty and wrapping up with a lingering bitter finish.

THE STORY Mornington Peninsula's Red Hill Brewery has a well-established roster of limited releases that come out month by month every year. All have their fans, but one is more hotly anticipated than all others, by a significant margin. That is their imperial stout, a genuine Aussie craft beer classic that pretty much sells out before it is even brewed. It has been around so long – and the brewers are forward-thinking enough to have put some aside – that occasionally they invite drinkers to join them for vertical tastings of multiple vintages, a veritable delight.

In recent years, they have released an even more limited version called the Double Barrel Imperial Stout, which has been aged in old whisky barrels. The 2013 version, which saw the beer rise to 10.2 per cent in the oak, was a triumph, adding warmth and further complexity to a very fine beer.

Brewer's food match
Cashel Irish blue cheese, chocolate

Availability
Seasonal (June–July)

Where to find it
Quality bottle shops and bars in Victoria, New South Wales and Queensland

Brewery and cellar door location
88 Shoreham Road, Red Hill South, Victoria

Brewery website
www.redhillbrewery.com.au

Extra Stout

REHN BIER

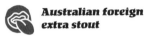 **Australian foreign extra stout** **6.0%**  **11-14°C** **Keller**

TASTING NOTES This viscous, almost oily extra stout is a luscious warming beast of a beer. It leans towards sweeter chocolate malts with a touch of coffee sharpness, with a mouthfeel that is rich, full, smooth and long-lasting.

THE STORY The Australian beer landscape is changing so fast that even someone who spends their entire life immersed in it can struggle to keep up with new arrivals. I first came across Rehn Bier while compiling this book, when the husband-and-wife team behind the Barossa Valley–based 'nano' brewery, Brenton and Robyn Rehn, made contact and sent some beers. They only started out at the tail end of 2012 and have an environmentally friendly, locally focused approach that sees them use all Australian ingredients and sell pretty much all their beer within 100 km of their home.

The three beers they sent, a Belgian-style tripel, an English-style extra special bitter and this extra stout, are all solid, with the last of them particularly impressive and an indication of the standards some brewers are achieving, even on the tiniest of setups.

Brewer's food match
Lamb shanks with mash, beef casserole, or bitter chocolate tart

Availability
Year round

Where to find it
Barossa Farmers Market, various outlets in the Barossa Valley; selected outlets in Adelaide

Brewery location
Angaston, South Australia

Brewery website
www.rehnbier.com.au

Southwark Old Stout

SOUTH AUSTRALIAN BREWING COMPANY

 British imperial stout   **7.4%**    **7-10°C**    **Dimpled handle**

TASTING NOTES This old-timer is surprisingly light on its feet for a beer registering 7.4 per cent alcohol. Dark brown with a reddish tint and tan head, it offers up mocha, vanilla and creamy chocolate aromas, with flavours dominated by chocolate, accompanied by some cola, cacao, even saltiness, before the bitter roast malt sign-off that lingers long on the palate.

But survive it does, packaged within quite possibly the most old-fashioned clothing of any currently available Aussie beer; a reminder of just how good some beers were well before 'craft beer' entered the lexicon, and a solid stout that holds its own in today's rapidly evolving marketplace.

THE STORY One of those beautiful and ever-so-rare (or perhaps beautiful *because* they're so rare) anomalies in the world of Australian beer, the Southwark Old Stout is a beer that by all rights should no longer exist. Somehow this much-loved, rich, dark beauty survived decades of homogenisation within the Australian beer industry throughout the twentieth century, as well as takeovers of the company that created it, the South Australian Brewing Company, established in Adelaide in 1859.

Brewer's food match
Rich desserts (e.g. chocolate cakes, toffee- or caramel-topped puddings)

Availability
Year round

Where to find it
South Australia only

Brewery and cellar door location
107 Port Road, Thebarton, South Australia

Stark Raven Dry Oatmeal Stout
SEVEN SHEDS

 Dry oatmeal stout   **6.7%**   **8-12°C**   **Straight-sided pint**

TASTING NOTES This medium-bodied, dark-brown oatmeal stout is a robust affair, eschewing the softer end of the darker malt spectrum for aromas and flavours that are of the roasted, bitter chocolate kind. There's a distinct woody nature to it too, and a touch of nuts, giving it solid, old-school appeal.

THE STORY Like many Tasmanians, Willie Simpson and partner Catherine Stark are great supporters of local produce and their surrounding region. They grow their own hops next to their cellar door, including one variety, Leggett, that is no longer grown anywhere else; have forged a strong and ongoing relationship with Lark Distillery; and, for their 200th brew, Platypus 200, featured cocoa from Anvers Confectionery, ginseng from 41° South, and quinoa from Kindred Organics – all small businesses that call northwest Tasmania home. It's a practice first seen in this fine winter seasonal, which features organic oats from nearby Elgaar Farm.

The couple's dedication to promoting the fascinating array of small producers in their backyard has seen them play a key role in launching the Cradle to Coast Tasting Trail, a handy way of discovering why so many people from all over the world have decided to end their travels there.

Brewer's food match
Bruny Island oysters

Availability
Seasonal (April–August approx)

Where to find it
Selected Tasmanian outlets; on tap at New Sydney Hotel, Hobart

Brewery and cellar door location
22 Crockers Street, Railton, Tasmania

Brewery website
www.sevensheds.com

Vanilla Milk Stout

THIRSTY CROW BREWERY

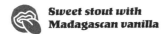 **Sweet stout with Madagascan vanilla** **5.2%**  **10°C** **Pint glass**

TASTING NOTES Its very name hints clearly at much of what to expect, with lactose adding a sweet, milky creaminess and vanilla from Madagascar to the fore. But this beer from Wagga's Thirsty Crow wouldn't have become the cult classic it is without the chocolate and coffee characters that round out this deeply dark and decadent stout.

THE STORY Thirsty Crow's founder, Craig Wealands, had not long returned to his hometown of Wagga before setting up a brewery with his family, having honed his brewing skills at other breweries in Queensland and New South Wales. He'd never brewed a milk stout before making this beer, one of the first through his brewpub setup, either. Yet three months after opening Thirsty Crow, the Vanilla Milk Stout picked up a trophy at the Australian International Beer Awards and announced the fledgling brewery to the wider beer world.

The venue has gone on to become a popular hub for quality beer, food and live music in the city, while Craig's frequently inventive beers are in high demand in Sydney and, when available, further afield. Availability should become less of an issue as he has been seeking a site for a second, high-volume production facility since 2013.

Brewer's food match
Crème brulee with chilli chocolate mousse

Availability
Year round

Where to find it
Thirsty Crow Brewery

Brewery and cellar door location
31 Kincaid Street, Wagga Wagga, New South Wales

Brewery website
www.thirstycrow.com.au

Belgian Styles

It feels somewhat criminal to be lumping all Belgian beers together in one place. It's almost like writing a book on wine and having a separate chapter for every red grape varietal and then one chapter for white wines.

The beers that come from Belgium encompass many of the most unique styles created in the drink's millennia-long history. What's more, they are held in high regard in Belgium itself. When the world's greatest beer writer, the late Michael Jackson, recorded an episode on Belgian beer for his classic TV show, *Beer Hunter*, it was entitled 'The Burgundies of Belgium' in recognition of beer's gilded position there, where beer rather than wine frequently takes pride of place at the dinner table.

While Belgian brewers do produce straightforward lagers, including volume shifters like Stella Artois, it is their kaleidoscopic array of fruity, spicy, complex, sour, intense and deeply rewarding ales that warrants the admiration of beer aficionados the world over. A tour of Belgium's classic breweries, many of them found within monasteries, is nothing less than a pilgrimage for many.

Belgian witbiers (literally 'white beers') are covered in the chapter on wheat beers. Other styles native to the country include Belgian pale and blond ales, golden ales of varying strength, saisons, dubbels, tripels and quadrupels, plus a range of unique sours: lambics, which, when multiple vintages are blended, create gueuzes; fruit beers such as kriek and framboise that add cherries and raspberries respectively to lambics; and Flanders red and brown ales (or 'Oud Bruin').

There are entire tracts written about each of these styles, so any summary here can only hope to be the briefest of introductions to entice you to explore Belgium's wonderful and unique beer heritage. What can be said is that, for the most part, unlike the vast majority of their New World peers, traditional Belgian brewers are less interested in showcasing hops than in creating beers of incredible complexity through the use of malt (often in combination with specialty sugars) and a range of idiosyncratic yeasts.

A common thread found through most Belgian pale ales, golden ales, dubbels, tripels and quadrupels is the fullness of their malt profile and a distinct fruitiness (ranging from raisins and plums to bananas), sometimes enhanced by spicy characteristics, that is obtained from the yeasts used. Another is the skill of the country's brewers in creating beers that are initially sweet and full in body yet finish remarkably dry, which is key to their drinkability.

Dubbels are potent dark ales typified by characteristics such as chocolate, caramel and dark fruits that are usually around 6 per cent or 7 per cent ABV. Tripels are lighter in colour, usually stronger in alcohol, and often display citrusy characters alongside peppery spices. Quadrupels, often referred to as Belgian dark strong ales, sit at the top of the chain, regularly greater than 10 per cent in alcohol content and offering incredible depth of flavour, which is again typified by sweet malts, dark fruits and Christmas cake–like spices.

Many of the finest examples of dubbels, tripels and quadrupels are regarded as among the greatest beers on the planet. And many of them are brewed by monks. This includes those at the ten monasteries bearing the Trappist accreditation, which must adhere to strict criteria. There are six in Belgium and one each in the Netherlands, Germany, Austria and the US, and they include some of the most iconic names in the world of brewing, such as Chimay, Orval, Westvleteren and Rochefort.

When it comes to sours, you enter another world altogether. At the most basic level, there are two main approaches taken by Belgian brewers. Those creating lambics and gueuzes leave their wort (see the section on the brewing process on page 20) in large, wide, shallow open vats to ferment with wild yeasts native to the area in which the brewery is based. They also pick up bacteria living within the brewery, resulting in uniquely sour ales with characteristics often defined as 'barnyard', 'horse blanket' or 'wet dog'. It is worth noting that brewers of such beers use hops that are several years old and boil them for up to six hours to ensure that they impart no flavour or aroma upon the finished beer – quite a distinction from most craft brewers.

When it comes to beers such as Flanders reds and browns, the process involves creating base beers that are often rich and malty, then ageing them within old wooden casks. These casks contain wild bacteria such as *Brettanomyces*, *Lactobacillus* and *Pediococcus*, which in their own way can add sour or acidic elements to the sweet and fruity characteristics already present, creating wonderfully complex finished beers that can present vinous and fortified-wine characters, too. More often than not, the brewers will blend various vintages or the contents of different barrels before packaging and releasing their beers.

Add saisons and bieres de garde, farmhouse ales that originate in the Wallonia region of France and Belgium and which are typically fruity and spicy (with saisons lighter and zesty, bieres de garde stronger and darker) and you have undoubtedly the most wildly varied collection of beers of any country in the world.

In Australia, brewers have attempted to create pretty much all of these styles, with a growing interest in sour beers in the past year or two. To date hardly any have been packaged, although look out for beers bearing the Bentspoke name as Richard Watkins, who made his name creating all manner of intriguing barrel-aged beers at Canberra's Wig & Pen Tavern, embarks on his own unique mission.

Over the coming pages you will find some fine interpretations of many of the styles listed above. There are also some New World twists upon the styles, usually involving the addition of huge amounts of hops, while you will find many more small-batch Belgian beers released as draught-only by local brewers. It is also worth noting that other styles of sour beer are beginning to appear from the more experimental Australian brewers. These are Berliner weisse and gose, both of which originate in Germany.

LA SIRENE SAISON

BRIDGE ROAD BREWERS/NØGNE Ø INDIA SAISON

MURRAY'S CRAFT BREWING PUNK MONK

Dubbel

BLACK HEART BREWERY

 Belgian dubbel   **7.4%**   **10-13°C** **Goblet**

TASTING NOTES In keeping with his home-brewing background, Black Heart head brewer Robin Brown always strives to create beers true to established guidelines. Some achieve greater success than others, with this Belgian dubbel one of those successes: a deep ruby-brown beer with a mocha head and excellent carbonation, in which vanilla aromas lead to flavours of chocolate, dark fruits and treacle.

THE STORY As backstories go, there are few as colourful as that of Black Heart Brewery. That it was set up by an award-winning home brewer is nothing out of the ordinary. That said home brewer is also a cardiac surgeon, who is assisted by a cardiac perfusionist who also works within Melbourne's hospitals, is rather unique. Add in the fact that

their tiny brewery is built in a shed next to the swimming pool in the surgeon's Brighton back garden, and you've got a set-up unlikely to be repeated anywhere in the world.

The brewing ethos is one based around creating traditional beers to style, and rarely does a month pass without a new release from Robin Brown and Brad Schultz. You'll find English, American, German and Belgian styles under the Black Heart banner, with this rich dubbel the most recent standout from their ever-lengthening line-up.

Brewer's food match
Smoked or barbecued meats, stews, steaks; washed-rind abbey-style cheeses; milk chocolate, truffles, bread and butter pudding

Availability
Seasonal/limited release

Where to find it
Full list of stockists available on website

Brewery location
Brighton, Victoria

Brewery website
www.blackheartbrewery.com.au

B2 Bomber
BRIDGE ROAD BREWERS

 Black Belgo-Indian ale 8.3% 9°C  IPA glass

TASTING NOTES This collision of styles has evolved over its three releases; last time out, a huge increase in the hopping rate pushed its resinous, fruity hops to the fore and nudged the Belgian esters into the background a little. There's also plenty of roasted malt flavour, in this unique combination of two – maybe even three – beers in one.

THE STORY Bridge Road's Ben Kraus has never been afraid to push the boat out when marking the brewery's birthday each year. In the past, the anniversary has been marked with a delicious barrel-aged imperial porter, and twists on his regular beers. One birthday beer has proved a stayer, however. The B2 Bomber mixes the hopping regime of an IPA with a fruity Belgian yeast and the sort of roasted, dark malts one would expect to find in a porter or stout. The first batch proved so popular that it has been brewed twice more since, each time souped up a little from the last. Black Belgian IPAs almost seem to have become a thing now, but when the B2 first took to the skies there was nothing of its ilk anywhere on the horizon.

Brewer's food match
Rich meat or oily dishes; anything charred; or just skip the food and have with cigars

Availability
Seasonal, anniversary edition

Where to find it
Specialty craft beer outlets

Brewery and cellar door location
50 Ford Street, Beechworth, Victoria

Brewery website
www.bridgeroadbrewers.com.au

India Saison

BRIDGE ROAD BREWERS/NØGNE Ø

 India saison 7.5% 8°C IPA glass

TASTING NOTES Two beers in one here. The India Saison opens up with a powerful hit of grassy and tropical fruit aromas from heavy use of Australian hops. Later on, particularly as the beer warms, they are joined by the steadily building influence of the spicy, herbal, even tart characteristics of the Belgian yeast.

THE STORY Bridge Road's Chevalier Saison, one of Australia's first and finest farmhouse ales, could well be on this page, but instead I opted for this twist on the style, a twist that is carried off with such panache that what was intended as a one-off collaboration is now brewed regularly on both sides of the planet.

Beer's recent renaissance has seen many experimental beers created, and just as many discarded as fads.

Few experiments have led to such spectacular results as this. The first of what has become an ongoing series of collaborations between the Australian and Norwegian breweries, the India Saison came about due to the two head brewers' shared love of the saison style and was brewed when Bridge Road's Ben Kraus visited Grimstad. Hop Products Australia sent a pack containing some of their newest hop varieties to the brewery and far more were thrown at the beer than, quite possibly, any saison before. The result is something that on paper perhaps shouldn't have worked (and there have been highly hopped saisons since that don't), but in this case it did – in spades.

Brewer's food match
Rich, spicy or oily dishes

Availability
Seasonal, two or three times a year

Where to find it
Specialty craft beer outlets

Brewery and cellar door location
50 Ford Street, Beechworth, Victoria

Brewery website
www.bridgeroadbrewers.com.au

Hagenbeck Belgian IPA

CHEEKY MONKEY BREWERY

 Belgian/American IPA **5.8%**  **8-10°C** **Tulip glass**

TASTING NOTES Having opted for this quirky style as their flagship, Cheeky Monkey made it a good one. The first thing that hits you from this copper-coloured beer is its grapefruit-dominated pop aromas, with some bubblegum from the Belgian yeast character poking through later. There's some sweetness and a touch of spice to taste, but that's secondary to the hops, building to a distinctly bitter crescendo.

THE STORY It took the team behind Cheeky Monkey Brewery rather longer than most to go from deciding to build a brewery to actually brewing beer and opening the doors to the public. And that's saying something in an industry in which it pays to add at least six months to whenever a prospective brewer tells you they plan to be operational. A very public spat with their Margaret River neighbours, the biodynamic winemakers Cullen Wines, who argued that brewing yeast could pose a potential danger to their practices, made other brewers' issues with council red tape or delayed deliveries of stainless steel seem trivial by comparison.

When the green light was finally granted, they had a local boy recently returned from Scottish craft beer behemoths Brew Dog at the helm. And while Jared 'Red' Proudfoot has since moved on to start a new brewing project entitled Pirate Life, he left behind Hagenbeck, the Belgian IPA that he designed as Cheeky Monkey's quirky flagship beer.

- -

Brewer's food match
Versatile, but rich blue cheese on sourdough is particularly good

Availability
Year round

Where to find it
Perth metro area and southwest Western Australia

Brewery location
Margaret River, Western Australia

Cellar door
4259 Caves Road, Wilyabrup, Western Australia

Brewery website
www.cheekymonkeybrewery.com.au

- -

Raging Flem Belgian IPA

FERAL BREWING

 Belgian IPA   7.8%    7°C   Spiegelau IPA glass

TASTING NOTES A frothy fiesta in each copper-coloured glass, this, from the moment a dense cloud of punchy citrusy American hops merges with sweet malts and hints of banana to assault the drinker's nose. The flavour is an equally full-on blend of sweet caramels and resinous hops, leaving little room for the Belgian yeast character to show through, although it does contribute to the voluptuous mouthfeel.

THE STORY As beer names go, there can be few in the world of Australian beer that are less enticing than Raging Flem. Certainly when heard rather than read, it brings to mind a furious, red-faced man wrestling with a particularly vicious frog in his throat. As it is, the name has rather more thoughtful, though still colourful, origins.

The beer, a Belgian IPA, was set to be launched at a Feral event at trailblazing Melbourne venue The Local Taphouse, and the head brewer invited attendees of said event to come up with a name. The winner was conjured by the beer industry's ubiquitous Professor Pilsner, Pete Mitcham, with nods to the raging seas the original IPAs crossed to reach India, and to the Flemish region of Belgium that is home to some of the country's finest beers.

That said, with the beer packing Feral's usual no-holds-barred American hop hit, a big, mouth-coating body and Belgian undertones, it's one for which anything tamer than Raging Flem just wouldn't have worked.

Brewer's food match
Chinese-braised beef short ribs

Availability
Year round on tap; seasonal in bottle

Where to find it
On tap and at good bottle shops
Australia-wide

Brewery and cellar door location
152 Haddrill Road, Baskerville,
Western Australia

Brewery website
www.feralbrewing.com.au

Pobblebonk Saison

FORREST BREWING COMPANY

 Saison de miel   **7.0%**   **Your preferred temperature**   **Goblet**

TASTING NOTES This seasonal release from the tiny Otway Ranges brewery is a delightfully zesty and refreshing drop. A saison de miel featuring locally sourced strawberry orange clover honey, it offers up citrus, spice, honey and pepper from start to finish.

THE STORY Brother-and-sister duo Matt and Sharon Bradshaw took over the former general store in the tiny township of Forrest in the Otway Ranges and have turned it into one of Australia's quaintest little microbreweries. As much part of the local mountain-bike scene – it's nestled alongside some of the country's finest tracks – as it is part of Victoria's rural microbrewing scene, its kitchen offers up dishes as rustic as the surrounds in which they are served,

as well as a range of beers with names inspired by the local region.

Their finest release to date is this saison de miel (a French/Belgian farmhouse-style ale brewed with honey), which is brewed annually and was first released in 2013. Named after a local frog and brewed with locally sourced honey, it's a wonderfully zesty take on a style much suited to the Australian climate.

Brewer's food match
Cedar house-smoked salmon with deconstructed tartare

Availability
Seasonal (autumn)

Where to find it
Selected independent outlets in Melbourne, Geelong and the Great Ocean Road region; preferred outlet Blackhearts & Sparrows

Brewery and cellar door location
26 Grant Street, Forrest, Victoria

Brewery website
www.forrestbrewing.com.au

Saison
LA SIRÈNE

 Saison **6.5%** **4°C**  **Tulip glass**

TASTING NOTES A beer that is no less stunning to look at in the glass than it is to taste, this is a truly effervescent beast that pours a cloudy light orange with a steepling, bulbous white head from which waft citrus and orange-blossom aromas underpinned by a touch of spice. Sweet, honey-like malts mix with spices in the mouth before finishing refreshingly tart and dry.

THE STORY Costa Nikias and James Brown met while studying winemaking. The former is a brewing consultant, the latter a microbiologist, and they bonded over a joint love of Belgian beers. Ultimately, this love led them to create La Sirène, a brewing company dedicated to creating nothing but French- and Belgian-inspired ales.

'Dedication' is the appropriate word too, as before creating their first beer they scoured the region from which the saison style originates until they found a yeast and a recipe that they were able to buy from a family that was no longer brewing commercially. At the second try the yeast made it safely to Australia, where it is kept in James's lab until the time comes to culture it up ready for the next brew. Their attention to detail paid off, as their saison is probably the best in Australia, and has been followed by a few well-received variants. As of late 2013 they have their own brewery too, which should ensure that far more people get to experience the delightful fruits of their labour of love.

Brewer's food match
Fish, chicken and spicy Mexican food

Availability
Year round

Where to find it
Australia-wide – refer to the stockist list on the La Sirène website

Brewery location
Alphington, Victoria

Brewery website
www.lasirene.com.au

Mad Abbot Tripel
THE LITTLE BREWING COMPANY

 Tripel **9.5%** **8-10°C**  **Trappist goblet**

TASTING NOTES As fine a Belgian tripel as you'll find in Australia, this Mad Abbot beer is a light, golden ale overflowing with honey, citrus and stone fruit aromas, with a touch of soft spice in there, too. On the palate it's full and creamy, with some warming sweet alcohol and a dry, spicy, peppery finish in a beer that conceals its 9.5 per cent alcohol well.

THE STORY Little Brewing Company's head brewer, Warwick Little, has long been fascinated by Belgian ales. As well as the short-lived Abbey Ale from the brewery's early days, there have been three other Belgian-inspired releases, all of which have a strong claim to a place in this book. His dubbel is a complex mix of chocolate, plums, raisins, vanilla and spices. The

Christmas Ale that was debuted in 2013, essentially a Belgian quadrupel inspired by one of the world's greatest beers, Rochefort 10, is an equally multifaceted delight that belies its 11.3 per cent alcohol content and isn't shamed by being mentioned in the same breath as its role model.

But I will settle for their tripel, as it was my introduction to the Port Macquarie brewery and remains the best Australian interpretation of the style.

Brewer's food match
Pungent and ripe soft cheese plate

Availability
Year round

Where to find it
Good independent bottle shops

Brewery and cellar door location
Unit 1/58 Uralla Road, Port Macquarie, New South Wales

Brewery website
www.thelittlebrewingcompany.com.au

Punk Monk

MURRAY'S CRAFT BREWING

 Belgian strong pale ale 7.5% 4-8°C  Chalice

TASTING NOTES An elegant, delicate charmer of a beer, this melange of multiple Belgian styles is one of Murray's head brewer Shawn Sherlock's personal favourites. It's easy to see why, with gentle fruity esters and soft spices leading into a silky-smooth, sweet then dry beer that caresses the palate. A superb, subtly complex beer ideal for the dining table.

THE STORY It's hard to pin down Murray's specialty. The Port Stephens brewery releases a fine range of hop-forward beers (see the Icon elsewhere in this book, then include the likes of Spartacus Imperial IPA and Vesuvius, too). It regularly puts out three high-quality imperial stouts every winter. And it has multiple top-notch Belgian-style ales to its name as well. The exquisite Grand Cru could easily have made this book as Murray's Belgian representative, perhaps even the Libertine Saison (although that's pitched as French-inspired), but the Punk Monk pips them at the post.

Something of a hybrid of Belgian ale styles, brewed using three different yeast strains, it is a wonderfully subtle and delicate affair. In fact, despite the image of a monk wearing a lurid pink habit on its label, it is anything but punk in nature.

Brewer's food match
Ripe washed-rind cheese

Availability
Seasonal

Where to find it
On draught Australia-wide at good craft beer venues; bottled seasonally and available Australia-wide at good independent bottle shops

Brewery and cellar door location
3443 Nelson Bay Road, Bobs Farm, New South Wales

Brewery website
www.murraysbrewingco.com.au

Temptation

RED HILL BREWERY

 **Strong Belgian golden ale** 8.5% 6°C Goblet

TASTING NOTES This strong Belgian golden ale is another of Red Hill's once-a-year releases and possesses the subtle complexity unique to Belgian beers that makes for a fantastic food beer. Surprisingly 8 per cent, this cloudy, pale golden beer displays everything from a honey-like sweetness to sugar, pear and grapes, cardamom and white pepper.

THE STORY Red Hill Brewery is a great advert for the benefits of giving in to temptation. Karen and David Golding, inspired by overseas travels, decided to jack in their careers in Melbourne, head to the Mornington Peninsula and open the region's first microbrewery, complete with its own hop farm. The move, helped no doubt by the development of one of the most consistent beer ranges in Australia, has proved a smart one.

Their beers, including this fine Belgian ale that can also be picked up on occasion in gin barrel–aged form, are in such demand that in 2012 they opted to close their cellar door and restaurant to allow for expansion. The venue still opens on some weekends, when it never fails to pack out, while, as of the end of 2013, beer-loving tourists can rent the Golding's former home onsite and experience a snippet of life on a working brewery.

Brewer's food match
French washed-rind cheese

Availability
Seasonal (September–October)

Where to find it
Quality bottle shops and bars in Victoria, New South Wales and Queensland

Brewery and cellar door location
88 Shoreham Road, Red Hill South, Victoria

Brewery website
www.redhillbrewery.com.au

Elephant's Trunk

SEVEN SHEDS

 Belgian Trappist ale   7.0%   8-12°C   Goblet

TASTING NOTES A cracking dark Belgian ale, the Elephant's Trunk pours a dense ruby colour and steadily unveils a wealth of aromas and flavours – raisins, plums, chocolate, treacle, dark sugars, sweet spices – as the relatively high alcohol gently warms.

THE STORY Look down the long line of beers that Seven Sheds has brewed over its 200-plus batches and, almost to a man, they are based on styles native to the British Isles; of the core range, only this strong Belgian ale deviates from the norm. Yet the Railton brewery is far from a one-trick pony, with frequently fascinating experiments seemingly always on the go.

For a start, its full title is Seven Sheds Brewery and Meadery; in the early days, if less so now, it released a series of meads and fruit melomels.

There have been beers brewed with 100 per cent peated distilling malt (Smokin' Bagpipes) and two beers that roped in the Spirit of Tasmania II ferry to take beer sealed in wooden barrels back and forth across the Bass Strait. (One re-created the journey the original India pale ales would make between the UK and India, the other was a reenactment of the first beer ever sent from the UK to Australia.) If you're lucky, some of all three may still be available at the cellar door.

Brewer's food match
Carbonade flamande

Availability
Year round

Where to find it
On tap at New Sydney Hotel, Hobart

Brewery and cellar door location
22 Crockers Street, Railton, Tasmania

Brewery website
www.sevensheds.com

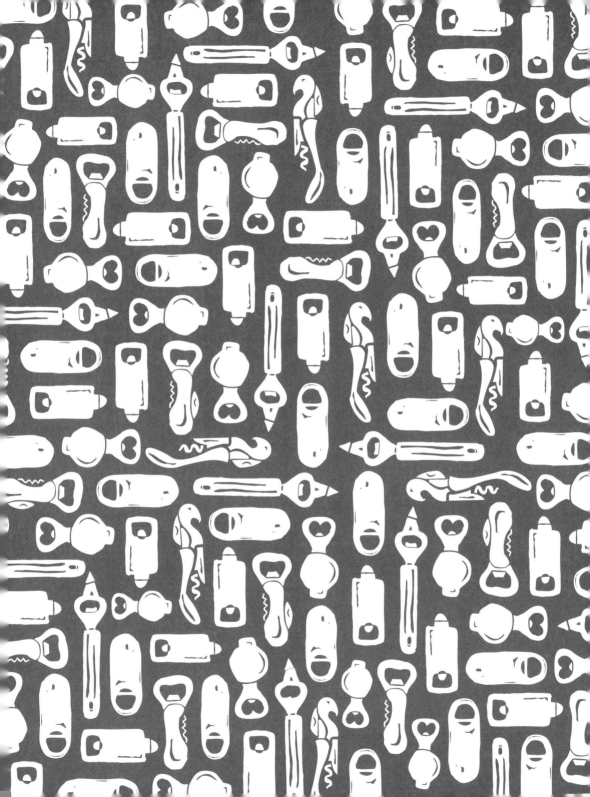

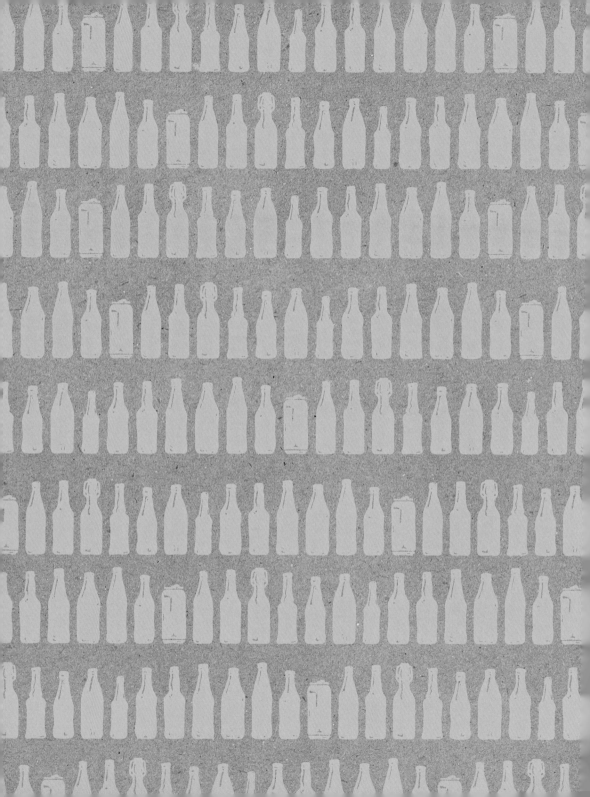

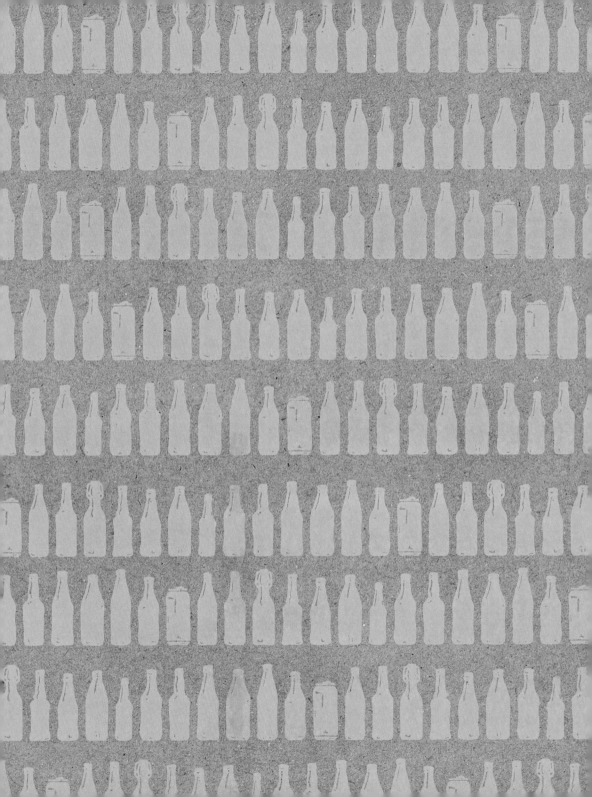

Wheat Beers

Wheat, both in malted and unmalted form, is used in a wide variety of beers. It can be used in beers such as golden ales to add a tartness of character and drying quality, and in some cases it's added in small percentages to aid head retention.

When talking about wheat beers as a category, however, it is generally understood to mean styles also referred to as 'white' beers that are characterised by the aromas and flavours derived from their yeasts. The two main families originate in Germany and Belgium.

In Germany, these weissebier come in a number of forms, with the most common being the cloudy Hefeweizen (literally translated as 'yeast wheat') the bright, filtered Kristalweizen, the dark Dunkelweizen ('dark wheat') and stronger, maltier variants called Weizenbock (literally 'wheat strong').

The unique yeast strains found in these beers, most famously those belonging to the world's oldest existing brewery, Weihenstephan, create distinctive fruity and spicy characters. These are usually described as banana, clove and even bubblegum. The beers also feature a high proportion of wheat malt in the grain bill, normally 50 per cent. Hop influence is barely noticeable, with these beers low in bitterness, too.

Belgian witbiers ('white beers') feature yeast strains that also create fruity, spicy and herbal aromas and flavours. They traditionally feature the use of adjuncts within the brewing process too, usually fruits and spices. Most common are ground coriander, Curaçao and citrus peel, although it is not unusual to find the likes of cardamom, star anise, pepper, cinnamon and others in witbiers. Again, there is up to 50 per cent wheat within the grain bill and hop presence is mild.

In the case of both German and Belgian styles, expect sweet malt flavours alongside those fruity, spicy characteristics and also a refreshingly dry finish. Some can even have a tartness, occasionally bordering on puckering.

With their light, fruity and refreshing nature, in many countries they are regarded as great warm-weather beers. Certainly that is the case in Australia, with brewers releasing witbiers and Hefeweizen as spring or summer seasonals. There are a number of good examples brewed here, and at one stage it appeared that almost every new microbrewery, especially in WA, would include one or the other as part of their core range.

You can also find a handful of beers categorised as American wheat beers. These use more neutral yeast strains – in other words, yeasts that give off no fruity or spicy characters as byproducts during fermentation – but still use high proportions of wheat, usually in combination with copious amounts of New World hops. There are also New World twists on traditional styles, such as highly hopped, higher alcohol witbiers or Weizenbock.

The past couple of years have seen a number of releases, usually to mark special occasions or as collaborations between different breweries, tagged as Hopfenweizenbock ('hops wheat strong'); the head brewer of Weihenstephan even created one especially for the Australian market to coincide with his visit to the country in 2014, using new Australian hop varieties to add a tropical nuance to one of his classic beers.

TOP OF THE HOPS

BURLEIGH BREWING HEF
RED HILL BREWERY WEIZENBOCK
GOODIESON BREWERY WHEAT BEER

HEF

BURLEIGH BREWING

 South German-style Hefeweizen   5.0%   6 °C   Weizenglass

TASTING NOTES The beer bearing the big, curly moustache on its label is a cloudy, unfiltered affair, full of body and awash with banana and clove aromas, possessing a citrusy tang to boot.

THE STORY When it comes to brewing heritage, the Germans have it in spades. They have the world's oldest continuous brewery, Weihenstephan, and brew their beers in accordance with the world's oldest purity law, the Reinheitsgebot. They are renowned for the technical quality of their brewing, and invented a number of styles of which they are the undisputed masters. So one can only imagine the looks on the German brewers' faces when the results in the German-style wheat beer category were announced at the 2012 World Beer Cup in San Diego.

Not only had a German brewery not taken first prize – the gold medal went to an Australian brewery. Not only an Australian brewery, but one from the Gold Coast, not necessarily the first place that springs to mind when thinking about craft beer. The HEF was that beer, and it has picked up trophies closer to home too, ensuring Burleigh's trophy cabinet shelves are among the most overburdened in the country.

Brewer's food match
Drink as an aperitif; also pairs well with almost all seafood and anything with bite

Availability
Year round

Where to find it
Southeast Queensland, available Australia-wide in selected liquor chains, independent bottle shops and a variety of bars and restaurants

Brewery and cellar door location
17A Ern Harley Drive, Burleigh Heads, Queensland

Brewery website
www.burleighbrewing.com.au

Vic Secret

EDGE BREWING PROJECT

 New World
wheat ale
 6.0%
 9°C
 Wooden tankard

TASTING NOTES Not your typical wheat beer, this one. Instead, it's a showcase for a relatively new Australian-developed hop variety, Vic Secret, with a full-bodied base beer created with wheat malt and oats acting as a platform for the hop's powerful, resinous, pineapple characteristics to shine.

THE STORY The Australian hop variety Vic Secret was destined for the chopping board by its creators, Hop Products Australia. After years monitoring it in their breeding program, they concluded that it didn't quite have what was required to make the cut. However, after it was used by Bridge Road in one of their annual wet hop harvest ales, they changed their minds and put it out commercially.

Edge jumped on it soon after its release and used it to create an Australian version of a beer they had originally brewed in New Zealand using Kiwi hops. Clearly the brewers behind Edge spotted the variety's potential and knew how to use it. When I asked Hop Products Australia boss Tim Lord to name the beer that best showcased Vic Secret, this was the one he named.

Brewer's food match
Lemon and herb chicken, shopska salad

Availability
Seasonal

Where to find it
Independent bottle shops and bars

Brewery and cellar door location
124 Railway Place, West Melbourne, Victoria

Brewery website
www.edgebrewing.com.au

White Ale

FERAL BREWING

 **Belgian witbier** **4.6%** **7°C** **Spiegelau wheat beer glass**

TASTING NOTES Feral's first beer, it was was inspired by the classic Belgian Hoegaarden and is an unfiltered, cloudy white ale brewed with coriander and orange peel. Expect spice and citrus on the nose with some zesty citrus flavours on the palate, too.

THE STORY Hop Hog may be the beer with which Feral has conquered the rest of Australia, but in its home state of WA it is its first beer, Feral White, that dominates. Based on Belgian witbiers, such as Hoegaarden, it's easy to see why it would find favour in the bars of Australia's hottest, driest state: brewed with 50 per cent wheat and 50 per cent barley, it's a clean, refreshing blend of gentle citrus and spice characteristics. More recently, to mark Feral's ten-year anniversary,

it evolved into one of the brewery's finest beers yet.

The White Hog combined the grain bill of Feral White with the aggressive hopping regime of the Hop Hog, as well as the former's Belgian yeast, to create a remarkably sessionable and delicious beer combining the best of the two. It's not the only Hop Hog variant worth hunting down, either. Keep an eye out for the Barrel Fermented Hog, or BFH, a version that spends time in new American oak before being packaged, and simply must be sampled whenever it appears on tap.

Brewer's food match
Fresh fruit salad

Availability
Year round

Where to find it
Australia-wide at good liquor stores and beer bars

Brewery and cellar door location
152 Haddrill Road, Baskerville, Swan Valley, Western Australia

Brewery website
www.feralbrewing.com.au

Wheat Beer
GOODIESON BREWERY

 Wheat beer 5.2% 6-8 °C **Balloon or weissbier glass**

TASTING NOTES This pours a cloudy, peachy yellow with a cloudlike, fluffy head. Pleasant soft spice and clove aromas mix with sweet malts and a touch of citrus on the nose. It has a full mouthfeel lifted by a spritzy carbonation, starting sweet and gently fruity before finishing refreshingly dry.

THE STORY The Australian microbrewing world is full of people who have decided to abandon their former careers and follow their passion for beer. There aren't too many for whom that former career was also brewing, but such was the case for Jeff Goodieson, who worked for Lion prior to opening his brewery in the McLaren Vale region with his wife, Mary.

Having swapped the corporate brewing world for a shed on a couple of acres south of Adelaide, they have set about cultivating a reputation for their classically styled beers, collecting four trophies at the 2012 Royal Adelaide Beer Show. Their spiced annual Christmas ale is one of the best festive beers you'll find in Australia while, of their core range, this wheat beer is the standout, as exemplary a re-creation of the German Hefeweizen style as you will find anywhere in Australia. You may well have to travel to South Australia to sample it, however, as, like many of their local peers, they rarely send beer over the border.

Brewer's food match
Asian-style food

Availability
Year round

Where to find it
Retails in South Australia only; can be bought online

Brewery and cellar door location
194 Sand Road, McLaren Vale, South Australia

Brewery website
www.goodiesonbrewery.com.au

Weizenbock

RED HILL BREWERY

 Weizenbock 7.9% 6°C **Tall wheat beer glass**

TASTING NOTES Fresh off the packaging line, this annual seasonal from the Mornington Peninsula's original microbrewery is a startlingly rich and sweet blend of toffee, banana and chocolate, backed up with some spicy hops and warming alcohol.

THE STORY A few years ago, Red Hill Brewery's co-owner Karen Golding expressed surprise at the popularity of this, one of their many high-quality annual seasonal releases. She had always viewed it as the oddball in their lineup, a strong, fruity, sweet, German-inspired style rarely seen Down Under. Indeed, wheat beers as a whole are something of a 'love it or hate it' category; I know many avid beer lovers who will say they appreciate a good wheat beer, but would never choose to drink one.

Yet the Weizenbock style – and occasional hoppy variants – have become more prevalent, often being brewed as collaborations with international brewers or as 'occasion' beers, with notable releases including the Unifikator between Temple Brewing and Weihenstephan and the Mountain Goat/Brooklyn Brewery Hopfweizenbock.

Brewer's food match
Pork knuckle roasted with spices and caramelised pears

Availability
Seasonal (September–October)

Where to find it
Quality bottle shops and bars in Victoria, New South Wales and Queensland

Brewery and cellar door location
88 Shoreham Road, Red Hill South, Victoria

Brewery website
www.redhillbrewery.com.au

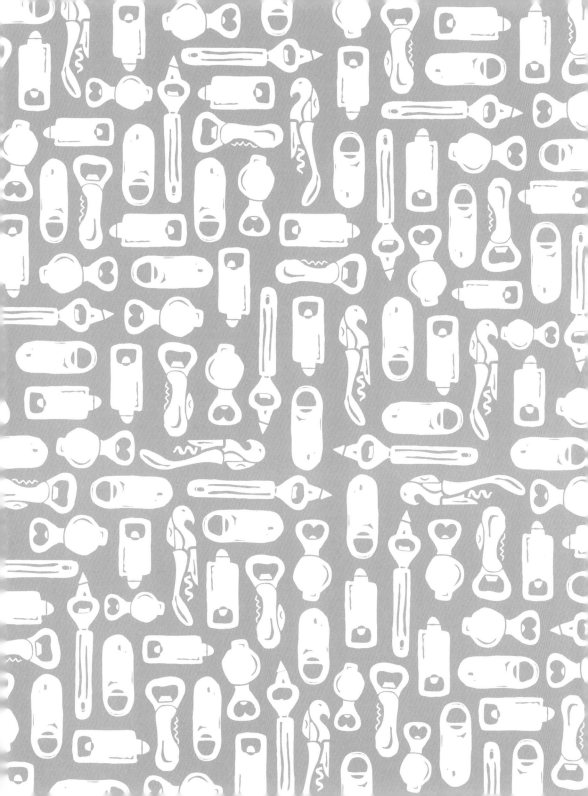

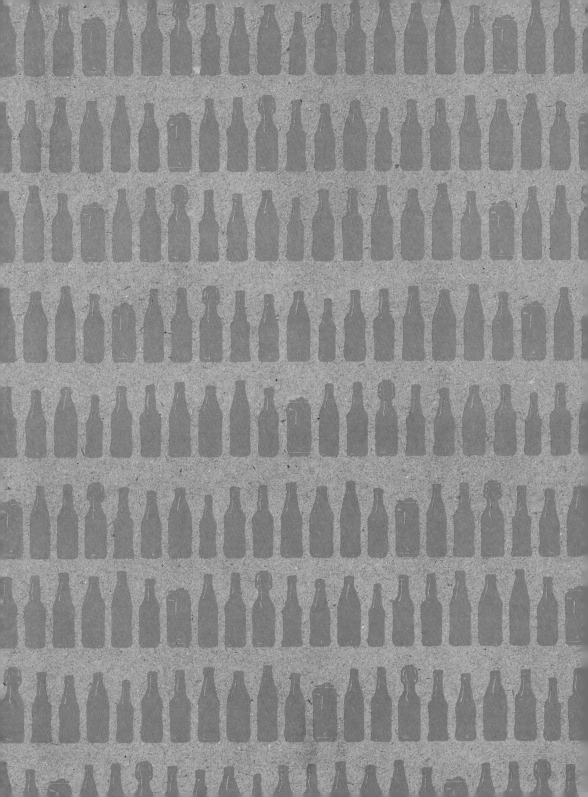

SPECIALTY
BEERS

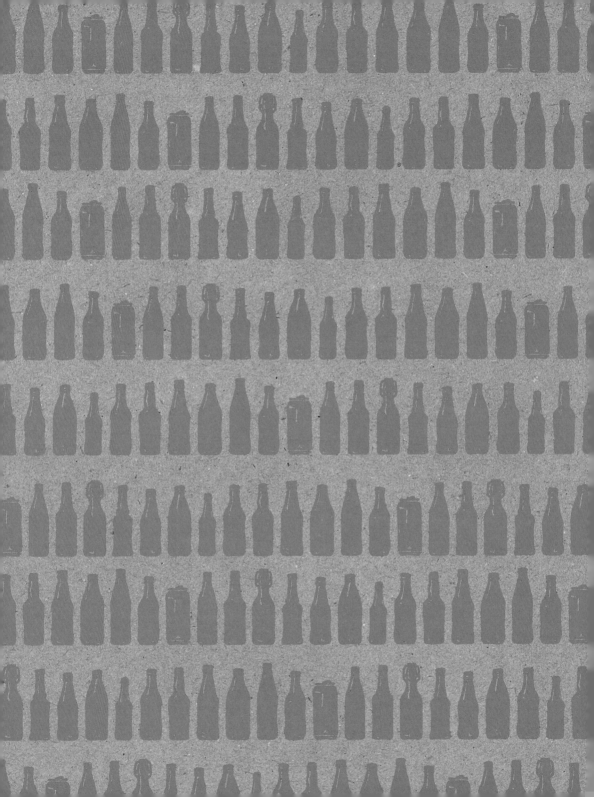

Specialty Beers

If there is a defining rule in the brave new world of craft brewing, it is that there are no rules. Every beer style created and recorded since beer's very earliest days thousands of years ago is there to be plundered and reinterpreted. Traditional beers are there to be reinvented and reinvigorated. Style categories are there to be thrown into a giant melting pot and turned into something new. And there is no limit to the ingredients you can use, the processes through which beer can pass before being consumed, or the vessels in which it can be fermented, conditioned, packaged or served.

While it is true that today's craft brewers are taking us back to before beer became little more than a commodity, many are also taking drinkers to places they've never been before. Grain and grape are being combined in beers that feature unfermented wine wort. Multiple brewers are coming together under one roof to combine their creative thoughts in one mash tun. There isn't a wooden barrel in existence – new French or American oak, wine, whiskey, cognac, akevitt, you name it – that a brewer somewhere won't have used to give their beer added complexity.

The spirit of innovation and experimentation is alive and well in Australia. Many of these often out-there beers are produced as one-offs and released only in draught format, so cannot appear here. But there are still plenty that you can find in bottles: barrel-aged barley wines, deliberately soured beers, one that uses volcanic stones heated in fire in the brewing process – even truly unique ales that blur the lines between beer and cider.

What most of the beers that you'll find in the coming pages share in common is that the brewers have used barrels at some stage before packaging and releasing them to the public. For centuries, all beers would be packaged and transported in, and served from, wooden barrels. Today, in almost every case, the journey from milled grain to finished beer takes place exclusively within steel vessels.

Contemporary brewers use wooden casks and barrels to achieve one or more of four outcomes. They may wish to add some oaky characteristics to their beer, as in Feral Brewing's fantastic Barrel Fermented Hog (also referred to as BFH), a semi-regularly brewed version of their all-conquering Hop Hog IPA that is fermented for a few days in fresh oak barrels.

In other cases, the goal is to pick up flavours or aromas from the previous inhabitant of the barrel, whether that is a wine or a spirit. Increasingly, and sometimes in combination with that goal, the intention is to allow wild yeasts and bacteria either already present in the barrel or added by the brewer to 'infect' the beer, thus giving it some of the sour or 'barnyard' characteristics described in the introduction to the Belgian beers chapter.

The final use for barrels is to allow slow and gentle oxidation of beer. Normally, brewers or vendors of beer want to avoid oxidation at all costs as, particularly in light, hop-forward beers, it can create unwanted flavours and aromas. But in stronger beers, particularly strong dark Belgian ales, imperial stouts and porters or barley wines, it can lead to desirable changes in the base beer. Oxidation can soften the roasty, harsher edges in big stouts and add caramel or vanilla notes. Likewise, in some beers it can lend them a fortified, sherry-like character.

Either way, whether with or without barrels, by sticking to beer's traditional four ingredients or by throwing everything including the kitchen sink into a brew, you will find beers out there limited by nothing more than a brewer's imagination. Not all of them will work, but often when they do they are fantastic experiences.

TOP OF THE HOPS

THOROGOODS BILLY B'S GOLDEN MALTED APPLE BEER
MOON DOG CRAFT BREWERY BLACK LUNG
REDOAK BREWERY SPECIAL RESERVE

Dark Ale

3 RAVENS

 Smoked ale   5.0%  6-8°C   Handled mug/stein

TASTING NOTES This homage to Bamberg wears its smokiness fairly delicately. The aromas coming off the chestnut-brown beer are of a sweeter nature: beechwood merging with caramel malts. And, while there are some pleasant soft German hop flavours and a touch of cola to taste, it's the smoke that returns to linger longest on the palate.

THE STORY Thornbury's 3 Ravens Brewery has enjoyed a colourful existence. Launched more than a decade ago by a bunch of engineers off the back of a beer brewed for a wedding, it soon secured a loyal following around Melbourne's inner north. In 2012, ownership squabbles meant it looked like the brewery would fold; it was even put up for sale, lock, stock and barrels (including those used to produce such delights as their Ale Noir and oak-aged Prussian porter). In the end, a compromise was reached, with Western Australians Mash Brewing riding to the rescue and allowing 3 Ravens to continue brewing, while also providing an eastern outpost to brew Mash seasonals.

A few things have survived intact from the early days: the Gothic look of their labels; the brewers' (in whatever incarnation) enduring love of obscure metal; and their Dark Ale. Taking a lead, like many of their beers do, from Europe, this is actually a rauchbier (literally 'smoked beer') inspired by Schlenkerla's range. One of Australia's first takes on the style, it remains a rarity a decade and more later.

Brewer's food match
Charcuterie

Availability
Year round

Where to find it
All good specialty beer outlets

Brewery and cellar door location
1 Theobald Street, Thornbury, Victoria

Brewery website
www.3ravens.com.au

Crown Ambassador

CUB

 Lager 9.6% 10-12°C  **Riedel Vinium Extreme Shiraz glass**

TASTING NOTES The brewery makes great play of the fact that the brewers travel to pick fresh Galaxy hop flowers the day before brewing this beer. However, being a beer that is designed to cellar for up to ten years and benefits from mellowing, by the time it is tasted those characteristics will have faded, leaving a rich, glowing-copper, dessert-like beer with caramel and toffee malts, stewed fruits, vanilla and a touch of drying oak to the fore.

THE STORY Thanks to the all-pervasive impact of *The Castle*, I find it almost impossible to think of CUB's annual luxury release, Crown Ambassador, without the phrase 'straight to the pool room' coming to mind. And while the nigh-on-$100-a-pop reserve lager,

which comes packaged in a voluptuous 750 ml bottle, itself housed within an exquisite, magnetically sealed silk-lined box, is unlikely to appear in the Kerrigans' home, it's certainly conceived with 'special gift for dad' in mind.

Strip away the price point, the lavish packaging and the fact that bottle number one is delivered to the queen, and what's left is a fine beer. Clocking in at around 10 per cent, each year's vintage tends to change a little, often with a small amount of a previous year's vintage blended back into the fresh brew, alongside an element that has been aged on oak. It's a marketing gimmick, for sure, but also one that gives CUB's top brewers a rare opportunity to create a beer that isn't destined for 'two slabs for $70' deals.

Brewer's food match
Intense-flavoured foods, including fine cuts of meat such as lamb, beef and pork, as well as oily fish like salmon or marron

Availability
Seasonal – launched once per year

Where to find it
Dan Murphy's Australia-wide and

selected quality independent bottle shops; restaurants and bars for a limited time after release

Brewery location
Abbotsford, Victoria

Brewery website
www.cub.com.au

Beelzebub's Jewels

HOLGATE BREWHOUSE

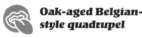 Oak-aged Belgian-style quadrupel   11.5%   10-12°C   Goblet or snifter

TASTING NOTES This barrel-aged, triple-fermented Belgian-style quadrupel is one of the most luxuriant Australian beers in which you can allow your palate to wade. I say 'wade', as the experience of sampling this dense, glistening, multifarious beast is akin to making one's way through a swamp, albeit one filled with gloriously rich and sweet caramel, toffee malts, stewed fruits and characteristics more commonly associated with fortified wines.

THE STORY However you choose to approach it, this beer has balls. It's the biggest in terms of alcohol content in the Holgate Brewhouse range. It's also the priciest of their beers. And it's the one that is longest in production. Then, of course, there's the tongue-in-cheek name and corresponding label artwork complete with a pair of (in)appropriately placed white dots.

Originally conceived when brewery owner Paul Holgate got his hands on some former pinot noir barrels from highly rated neighbouring winery Curly Flats, in its first incarnation it was merely an enhanced, barrel-conditioned version of the existing Double Trouble Belgian ale. When that experiment proved popular, they revisited the concept, only this time around creating a brand new beer from scratch, rather than re-fermenting an existing one. Now an annual Easter release, Beelzebub's Jewels has proved as popular with judges as beer geeks, collecting top medals in competitions both here and in New Zealand.

Brewer's food match
Gnocchi with three-cheese sauce; sticky date pudding

Availability
Year round, special reserve

Where to find it
Limited specialty stores, bars and restaurants; online

Brewery and cellar door location
79 High Street, Woodend, Victoria

Brewery website
www.holgatebrewhouse.com

Black Lung
MOON DOG BREWING

 **Barrel-aged smoky stout** **8.9%**  **10-12°C** **Goblet**

TASTING NOTES While the base beer remains essentially the same each time – a dense, black number from the heavier end of the stout flavour spectrum – this series of smoky, barrel-aged stouts features a different barrel each time: bourbon, whisky and rum so far. Each has presented its own characteristics, from the intense smoke and wood of the whisky to the beautifully integrated sweet fruits and drying oak of the rum barrel.

THE STORY In their first two years of operation, more often than not, any beer released by Melbourne's Moon Dog would be brewed once and once only. There have been exceptions to the rule and, in recent times, they have added a couple of core beers to their output, too. Among those exceptions is the Black Lung series. Ostensibly

a smoky, barrel-aged stout, each one has been a little different. The first was aged inside former bourbon barrels. The second was the fiercest yet, picking up a huge amount of character from the former whisky barrels in which it was aged. The third, released in 2013, took on elements of rum courtesy of barrels from the Hoochery Distillery.

They've gone bigger, too, notably with their Jumping the Shark cognac barrel-aged imperial stout weighing in above 15 per cent. First released in 2013, the first of what will be annual Jumping the Shark beers featured the Fonz from *Happy Days* on the labels. As for Black Lung, the fourth instalment is awaited with great anticipation – not something that can always be said about sequels this far down the line.

Brewer's food match
Red meat

Availability
Seasonal/annual release

Where to find it
Specialty venues Australia-wide

Brewery and cellar door location
17 Duke Street, Abbotsford, Victoria

Brewery website
www.moondogbrewing.com.au

Anniversary Ales

MURRAY'S CRAFT BREWING

 **Oak-aged barley wine** **10.0%**  **8-12°C** **Chalice**

TASTING NOTES This return to the Anniversary Ale's roots pours a ridiculously enticing copper colour. It's designed to age for a number of years, but even early on you can expect an abundance of complex flavours and aromas: rich caramel and nutty malts, dark and dried fruits, a touch of oak, complex hop flavours, warming alcohol and a big closing bitterness to finish.

THE STORY Murray's Anniversary Ale is one of four featured within this book that are a little like a Hollywood blockbuster series. There are many beers here that are annual releases, brewed once a year to a consistent recipe when the season or the brewer's whim deems appropriate. But this one, like the Ra series from Red Duck, Stone & Wood's Stone Beer and Moon Dog's Black Lung, has evolved with every release.

Originally a barrel-aged barley wine brewed to mark the brewery's first anniversary, over the years it has fluctuated in alcohol content, usually preferring an upward trajectory, and has also spent time in various types of oak, been blended and been inoculated with wild bacteria. The beer is released in seriously limited numbers every New Year's Day, with the 2014 release – Anniversary Ale 8 – seeing a return to where it all started, with the Belgian-influenced 15 per cent beers of recent years replaced with a 10 per cent barley wine.

Brewer's food match
Traditional Christmas lunch; soft, ripe blue cheese

Availability
Late December each year

Where to find it
Available from website and Australia-wide at good independent bottle shops

Brewery and cellar door location
3443 Nelson Bay Road, Bobs Farm, New South Wales

Brewery website
www.murraysbrewingco.com.au

Ra

RED DUCK BREWERY

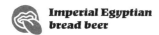 **Imperial Egyptian bread beer** **9.6%** **Any**  **Your favourite**

TASTING NOTES It's fair to say that Red Duck's series of Ra beers are to be experienced as much as enjoyed, and won't be for everyone. Each of the four hopless wonders has differed depending on the clutch of spices and other flavourings added to the mix, but they are united by their distinctly, almost puckeringly, sour nature and a thick, oily body.

THE STORY Red Duck's head brewer Scott Wilson-Browne is a keen student of beer's history. Particularly, it seems, how beer would have been brewed hundreds, even thousands, of years ago. He brews braggots, which are a blend of mead and strong ale with origins in medieval Britain; he's created a series of gruit stouts, inspired by the Middle Ages and brewed with such delights as homemade nettle goo and deliberately scorched grains; and he has created the Ra series of beers.

Inspired by the beverages created in ancient Egypt, he cultured yeast from a batch of sourdough bread to use in these beers that are brewed sans hops but with a cavalcade of spices, fruits and other oddities instead. For Ra #3 and #4, the yeast was cultured up from Ra #2. Tasting like anything from gelatinous, spicy breakfast juice to mouth-puckering, viscous goo, they are as oddball as they are unique, but have devout fans clamouring for each new iteration.

Brewer's food match
Hot-seared camel (or goat, kangaroo, ostrich or emu) fillets rubbed in olive oil and dukkah, and tossed with slivered almonds and raisins

Availability
Limited

Where to find it
Good boutique bottle shops, bars and restaurants

Brewery location
Ballarat, Victoria

Cellar door
11A Michaels Drive, Alfredton, Victoria

Brewery website
www.redduckbeer.com.au

Special Reserve
REDOAK

 Barley wine **12.0%**  **12°C** **Large chalice or large balloon**

TASTING NOTES A barley wine that is years in production, undergoing three separate fermentations and spending time maturing on oak, this unique creation has as much in common with an aged, fortified Pedro Ximenez as it does with beer. Luxuriant and velvety, this gently warming treat runs the gamut from vanilla, oak and chocolate through dates and raisins to its liqueur-like finish. Rare, expensive and stunning.

THE STORY Redoak, run by brother-and-sister pair David and Janet Hollyoak, is the Australian beer world's greatest enigma. Ever since David says he was hoodwinked into allowing 'spies' from one of the major breweries on a brewery tour (they were posing as home brewers), he has refused to open the doors of his Camden brewery to anybody. It means that the secrets of the country's most successful brewery in terms of global award success – this Special Reserve was named Supreme Champion at the UK's International Beer Challenge, one of many prestigious trophies collected in 2013 alone – remain just that: closely guarded secrets.

Whether the enigma will ever be unravelled – David says he will open the doors to the brewery once there are no more contracted taps in Australia – remains to be seen. But so many of the beers created by this passionate advocate for small, independent Australian brewers, who has been brewing since the age of fourteen, are so truly delicious that it's easy to forgive the shroud of mystery.

Brewer's food match
Best on its own as an aperitif

Availability
Year round

Where to find it
Cellar door only

Cellar door
201 Clarence Street, Sydney, New South Wales

Brewery website
www.redoak.com.au

Stone Beer

STONE & WOOD BREWING

 Dark **7.2%** **8°C**  **Snifter beer glass**

TASTING NOTES Each year's vintage tends to change slightly but, since jumping up in alcohol in 2012, the Stone Beers have been dark-brown beers with a blood-orange tint that exhibit subtle, spicy hops that leave the bulk of the heavy lifting to the caramelised malts: think toffee, chocolate, cocoa and treacle, all wrapped up in a typically balanced Stone & Wood package.

THE STORY Such has been the phenomenal success of Stone & Wood's Pacific Ale they have had little time to brew anything else – at least until the new, larger brewery was installed. A notable exception to the rule is this once-a-year Stone Beer, inspired by a technique from hundreds of years ago that sees volcanic rocks (that head brewer Brad Rogers has been lugging around since his brewing days in Fiji) heated in flames for hours on the brewery driveway before being lowered into the kettle in a metal cage where they caramelise the sweet, sugary water.

Their other notable side project is called The Mash Collective, which sees the Byron Bay brewers invite an eclectic collection of guests to help conceive a one-off beer – recipe, name, label design and all. Past contributors have included surfers, musicians, artists, tradies and John Birmingham, author of *He Died with a Falafel in His Hand.*

Brewer's food match
A rich, dark chocolate dessert, such as a self-saucing pudding or dark chocolate tart

Availability
Seasonal (brewed in March and released in May)

Where to find it
Selected bottle shops, restaurants and bars; see website for full list of stockists

Brewery and cellar door location
4 Boronia Place, Byron Bay, New South Wales

Brewery website
www.stoneandwood.com.au

Billy B's Malted Apple Beer
THOROGOODS

 **Fruit beer** **12.0%**  **Very cold** **Long glass**

TASTING NOTES This is a terrifically complex – even perplexing – oddball. Initially, you're met by a lambic-like sourness, some barnyard aromas, a sharp apple tang and a faint toffee sweetness on the nose before flavours that encompass rustic Normandy ciders, toffee apples, spice and a sour, citric-acid finish follow. Unique, and a barely credible 12 per cent, too.

THE STORY Outside home-brewing circles and specialist beer clubs there will be few Australians that know of Billy B's, even those who would consider themselves keen beer lovers. Yet among the global beer geek community, this apple beer from a tiny South Australian cider producer is one of the best-known beers from Australia: a genuine cult classic that visitors to the Burra cidery will mule to the farthest corners of the world.

Based upon a recipe handed down by one of the Thorogoods' relatives, who once lived in Yorkshire, it's a weird and wonderful, sweet and sour mix of apples and beer. The brewer is understandably coy about the technique by which Billy B's is created, and it's available in so few places that ordering direct from the brewery is your best bet. There's a 'stout' version too, although it lacks the complexity and intrigue.

Brewer's food match
Beer-battered Tasmanian blue eye and chips

Availability
Year round

Where to find it
Sydney: Bitter Phew; Queensland: Archive Beer Boutique, The Scratch Bar and Tipplers Tap; Victoria: Slowbeer, Sunshine Creek, The Alehouse Project, The Williamstown Fine Wine; Western

Australia: The International Beer Shop, Mane Liquor

Brewery location
Burra, South Australia

Cellar door
John Barker Street, Burra, South Australia

Brewery website
www.thorogoods.com.au

Derwent Aromatic Spelt Ale
TWO METRE TALL

 Naturally soured Tasmanian farmhouse ale

 5.2%

 6-8°C

 Large, tulip-shaped red wine glass

TASTING NOTES The initial waft of estate-grown hops is something of a false lead here. A clearer guide to what to expect are the citric lemon and musty aromas that accompany the hops. This light, pale-coloured ale, with a swirling haze within, is exceedingly dry and tart, with a puckering sourness that goes to work on the sides of your mouth.

THE STORY Two Metre Tall is nothing if not unique. Ashley and Jayne Huntington returned to Tasmania from France, where they had run a winery in the Languedoc region, bought 600 hectares of land in the Derwent Valley and, inspired by the local hop farms, abandoned winemaking for brewing, even growing their own hops. Experimentation with fruit juice in beer followed, as did some (not always intended) funky results. Emboldened rather than deterred,

Ashley embraced the wild side of brewing and now releases a number of soured, wild and barrel-aged beers.

Those that are packaged come in unique (literally) bottles detailing, in depth, the story of the brewery, the local region and, on individually numbered labels stuck over the cap, the exact ingredients in each beer as well as when they were brewed and bottled, as the couple looks to pass their fascination with beer and brewing on to the drinker.

Brewer's food match
Tempura prawns; navarin of spring lamb

Availability
Year round

Where to find it
Independent bottle shops; from website

Brewery and cellar door location
Farm Bar, 2862 Lyell Highway, Hayes, Tasmania

Brewery website
www.2mt.com.au

Hedgerow Autumn Ale

VAN DIEMAN BREWING

 Barrel-aged sour ale   **6.1%**   **12°C**   **Tulip glass**

TASTING NOTES While some local brewers head straight for 'lip-smacking' and 'mouth-puckering' when creating sours, the Hedgerow does it with elegance. This highly effervescent amber ale with a pinkish hue has some spritzy malt sweetness up front before a soft, lactic sourness comes in. The fruity, plummy character from the pinot noir that once inhabited the barrels is prominent too, making for a wonderful beer.

THE STORY Van Dieman founder Will Tatchell learned his brewing trade creating real ales in the UK before returning to his family farm in Evandale, south of Launceston. His training can be found throughout the Van Dieman range, which focuses predominantly on re-creating British styles, with his annual Little Hell ESB perhaps the pick of these re-creations.

The Hedgerow Autumn Ale is his most intriguing concoction, however. Initially, it was a lovely, rounded malty ale lifted by subtle forest fruit characteristics gained by racking the beer over rosehips, sloeberries and hawthorns he'd picked from around the farm for six weeks. Second time around, he increased the racking period to twelve weeks and aged some in pinot noir barrels, where the beer developed a soft sourness that elevated it to another level. Such was the acclaim for this new version of the Hedgerow that the barrels are rolled out for it every year.

Brewer's food match
Pan-fried duck breast with raspberries

Availability
Seasonal (autumn)

Where to find it
Select bottle shops around Tasmania; limited quantities are shipped to Melbourne

Brewery location
Evandale, Tasmania

Brewery website
www.vandiemanbrewing.com.au

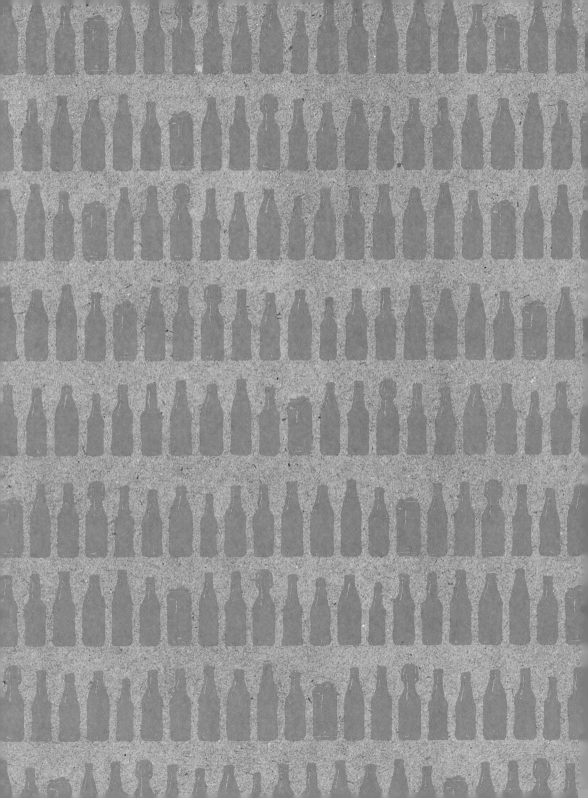

OTHER
BREWERIES

Other Breweries

Despite casting the net far and wide to include more than 80 different Australian breweries within the 150 beers featured in this book, there are still many more that don't appear in the list. At the latest count, there were more than 200 breweries and brewing companies across the country, with more opening every month. In fact, chances are that one will have just released its first beer in the time it's taken you to read this paragraph.

There are many that don't make the list for the simple reason that they don't package any of their beers. Just as some of the most interesting and spectacular beers released by Australian breweries are brewed once and once only or released in keg form only, there are dozens of breweries that have chosen not to invest in a packaging line.

Some are happy to serve their local market or the regulars and tourists that visit their brewpub or cellar door; others appreciate that the investment required to install a quality bottling line capable of delivering consistent, fault-free products is significant. It is a policy that is particularly common in Western Australia, where few have opted to even contemplate sending beer across the Nullarbor.

Over the coming pages, you will find a roundup of some of the breweries whose beers do not feature within the 150, but are well worth checking out, whether for their beers or the uniqueness of their brewpub or cellar door.

HUNTER BEER CO
WINE COUNTRY DRIVE, NULKABA, HUNTER VALLEY, NSW

An Australian microbrewery that calls a wine region home, Hunter Beer Co is located in the rather unique Potters Resort, built in and around a former brick and terracotta pot–making factory and its eye-catching kilns. Keith Grice and his team create one of the widest ranges of beers you'll find anywhere in the country. The best way to sample them is poured from the taps of the venue itself, where you're able to take a guided tour of the brewery.

BYRON BAY BREWERY
1 SKINNERS SHOOT ROAD, BYRON BAY, NSW

These days, Byron Bay is famed in craft beer circles after Stone & Wood came to town and created the Pacific Ale phenomenon. But even before they arrived there was a small brewery in town. One of the more unique setups in the Australian beer world, Byron Bay Brewery also features, among other things, a popular backpacker hostel. Since 2013, its head brewer is Scott Hargrave, who moved across town from Stone & Wood and has set about putting his own stamp on the beers.

ROCKS BREWING
160 BOURKE ROAD, ALEXANDRIA, NSW

As the name suggests, the team behind Rocks Brewing had Sydney's famed tourist precinct in mind for their brewery. But, despite opening Harts Pub there as the brewing company's original home, The Rocks proved less suitable for a brewery. A five-year search brought them to a warehouse unit in Alexandria where, early in 2014, they installed a high-tech brewery alongside an impressive bar, cafe and restaurant. Look out for a greater range of Rocks beers now they have total control of their brewing.

FORTITUDE BREWING COMPANY/NOISY MINOR
165-185 LONG ROAD, TAMBORINE NORTH, QLD

At the time of writing, preparations were underway for one of Queensland's newest brewing concerns to take over the former Mt Tamborine Brewery, a spectacular venue at the top of the town. Not only does it give them an expanded capacity but it means the two-brand brewery will have its own cellar door at which to showcase its broad range of beers. They are beers that come with an impeccable pedigree as head brewer Ian Watson was Shawn Sherlock's sidekick at Murray's (yes, really, Watson and Sherlock) before returning to his home state early in 2014.

SIX STRING BREWING
4/330 ENTRANCE ROAD, ERINA, NSW

Even by the usual standards, the length of time and the amount of red tape the founders of Central Coast's Six String Brewing faced to get up and running was ridiculous. Almost three years passed and four potential sites were considered before they opened their doors in 2013. Since then, they've wasted little time winning over the drinkers of the Central Coast, Newcastle and Sydney with their full-flavoured ales. As the name suggests, there are musicians among them, meaning visitors can frequently catch live music – sometimes featuring members of Six String – on a stage in front of the stainless steel tanks.

GREEN BEACON BREWERY
26 HELEN STREET, TENERIFFE, QLD

A first visit to Mountain Goat's brewery in Melbourne is an experience that never leaves you. The combination of bar and brewery in a towering industrial space is simple, but works so well. It's an experience that a pair of well-travelled schoolmates brought to Brisbane in 2013 in the form of Green Beacon. Their brewery lines one wall of a converted warehouse, a bar constructed from recycled spotted gum runs down the middle and, during opening hours, scores of happy drinkers surround it, tucking into a range of beers that is increasingly found on taps outside the venue, too.

NEWSTEAD BREWING COMPANY
85 DOGGETT STREET, NEWSTEAD, QLD

Not too long ago, locals were bemoaning the state of the Brisbane beer scene. These days it is a city transformed, with a rapidly growing number of incredibly diverse and high-quality venues and some fine new breweries too, with Newstead Brewing Company possibly the most eye-catching of all. It opened in 2013 in a converted bus depot/art gallery and combines brewery and bar with exquisite restaurant-quality food. Twelve taps pour eight of Newstead's own beers, plus a rotating selection of Aussies on the others.

BAROSSA VALLEY BREWING
2A MURRAY STREET, TANUNDA, SA

Having experienced great beer while working in the US, merchant banker Denham D'Silva couldn't find any on his return to Australia. So he did what any right-thinking person would do: he built his own brewery. Barossa Valley Brewing is located in the heart of wine country and takes full advantage of its surrounds. As well as regularly inviting winemakers to come and pit their produce against his at beer versus wine events, recently the grain and grape have been combined as one. In 2014, the brewery joined forces with Maverick Winds and David Franz Wines to create a beer that featured local semillon and riesling.

STEAM EXCHANGE BREWERY
GOOLWA WHARF PRECINCT, GOOLWA, SA

As of 2013 a real buzz was starting to build around microbrewing in South Australia, with a number of new breweries and brewing companies coming online. That said, there was already a handful dotted around the state, including Steam Exchange, something of a South Australian stalwart. They have been brewing beers for a decade in the converted railway goods shed on the wharf that overlooks Encounter Bay in Goolwa. It's as much a tourist destination as a craft brewery, and often has some quirky limited-release beers on offer alongside its core range.

WOOLSHED BREWERY
69 WILKINSON ROAD, MURTHO, SA

Proof that breweries can and do pop up anywhere and everywhere in Australia today, Woolshed Brewery is located in a converted shearer's shed on the banks of the Murray. It's been operating since 2009, using solar power, rainwater and other recycling techniques in its 1000-litre brewery to create beers that visitors get to enjoy on a veranda overlooking the river. On the beer front, it's probably best known for its Judas the Dark, a dark ale that features locally grown, native roasted wattleseed.

IRONHOUSE BREWERY
21554 TASMAN HIGHWAY, FOUR MILE CREEK, TAS

Tasmania's east coast possesses some of the most beautiful, if not the warmest, beaches in all of Australia. And one of them belongs to Ironhouse Brewery, or at least the White Sands Resort where it is based. This makes it one of the most stunning cellar doors you could wish to visit, with the aforementioned white sands of the beach just a two-minute stroll from the terrace adjacent to the brewery bar. For the most part, Ironhouse's beers are based on traditional European ales and lagers, although it is garnering quite a reputation in its home state for a Honey Porter brewed with distinctive leatherwood honey.

BULLANT BREWERY
46 MAIN STREET, BRUTHEN, VIC

For many years, it was possible to do a loop from Melbourne back to Melbourne that would take in the High Country without you ever needing to be too far from a brewery cellar door. Well, almost. Once you moved on from the tiny Sweetwater Brewery in Mount Beauty there was a hefty stretch over the top, through Bairnsdale and back to Mirboo North, before you hit Grand Ridge. Since 2011, however, beer lovers can slake their thirst in Bruthen, where Bullant Brewery serves up a range of traditional ales and lagers brewed onsite that can be enjoyed on the veranda looking out over the East Gippsland countryside, often with live music as an accompaniment.

THUNDER ROAD BREWING COMPANY
130 BARKLY STREET, BRUNSWICK, VIC

Thunder Road marches to the beat of its own drum: while most small Australian breweries tend to chase big flavours in ale-heavy ranges, the Brunswick brewery's ethos has always been to create the sort of clean and polished beers, usually lagers, that inspired owner Philip Withers when he landed at Chuckanut Brewery on a fact-finding tour of the US. They do so on one of the most high-tech microbrewery setups in Australia, which they occasionally open to the public. Withers' fascination with beer's history is manifested in a small but incredibly well stocked library in the historic Bluestone building that fronts their factory space.

COLONIAL BREWING COMPANY
OSMINGTON ROAD, BRAMLEY, WA

Colonial Brewing Company is one of the most impressive-looking brewery cellar doors you could wish to visit in Australia. Occupying a vast contemporary building on an even vaster plot of land in Margaret River, the brewery, bar, restaurant, kids' area and lawn are a great stop the family. For years, most of the beers were of a Germanic bent, although the palette has become ever more colourful recently. Under their 'Project Beer' banner, they have also been releasing beers with deliberately daft and non-descriptive titles, usually featuring the name Gary, with the belief that if a drinker has no preconception about what they're drinking then they will think about it more deeply.

DUCKSTEIN BREWERY
3157 CAVES ROAD, WILYABRUP, MARGARET RIVER, WA AND 9720 WEST SWAN ROAD, SWAN VALLEY, WA

Duckstein Brewery occupies two locations, both in popular Western Australian wine regions. And the two could hardly be more different. The one in Margaret River shares a site with Saracen Estates winery and is part of a spectacular, multimillion-dollar cellar door overlooking its own lake on the famous Caves Road. The Swan Valley site is a colourful, Bavarian-themed beer hall–type affair, complete with mechanical, lederhosen-wearing, moustachioed musicians. Both serve up a range of predominantly German-style beers alongside dishes inspired by that part of the world, too.

INDIAN OCEAN BREWERY
30 OCEAN FALLS BOULEVARD, MINDARIE, WA

A couple of years back, this brewery would not have featured here. As much the result of someone thinking, 'Hey, wouldn't it be a great idea to build a brewpub as part of this fancy new development?' as any desire to brew great beer, it has since been transformed. British brewer Dave Brough redesigned the brewhouse and its beers and, a year later, walked away from the Perth Royal Beer Show with the title of Best WA Brewery. Expect a range of traditional, usually European-inspired, ales and lagers.

LAST DROP BREWERY
507 NICHOLSON ROAD, CANNING VALE, WA

Last Drop is one of Australia's longest-established breweries. It was founded in 1992 by German master brewer Horst Kempf, who took a brewhouse from a medieval Bavarian village and imported it lock, stock and barrel to the Perth Hills. It specialises in traditional Bavarian beer styles, with the brewery now under the stewardship of Czech brewer Jan Bruckner. Surprisingly, given its heritage, the brewery, its bar and restaurant are located in a mock British Tudor tavern.

MATSO'S BREWERY
60 HAMERSLEY STREET, BROOME, WA

If you're going to build a brewery in Broome, you may as well make the brews tropical. Matso's occupies an enviable spot in a former Union Bank building overlooking the ocean. They do brew in their quirky onsite brewery, but most of the equally quirky beers bearing the Matso's brand and featuring local ingredients – Mango Beer, Chilli Beer, Ginger Beer, and so on – are now brewed offsite to meet demand.

THE MONK BREWERY & KITCHEN
33 SOUTH TERRACE, FREMANTLE, WA

This brewpub setup is turning into something of a training ground for top-notch brewers. A stream of locals (and the odd import) has taken up the reins on its small but expanding system and tested their talents on some highly polished and frequently trophy-winning beers. When they move on, most have a tendency to turn up down the road at Colonial Brewing Company in Margaret River, but not before leaving behind a few excellent beers in the Monk recipe book.

INDEX

Published in 2014 by Hardie Grant Books

Hardie Grant Books (Australia)
Ground Floor, Building 1
658 Church Street
Richmond, Victoria 3121
www.hardiegrant.com.au

Hardie Grant Books (UK)
Dudley House, North Suite
34-35 Southampton Street
London WC2E 7HF
www.hardiegrant.co.uk

A Cataloguing-in-Publication entry is available from the catalogue
of the National Library of Australia at www.nla.gov.au

150 Great Australian Beers
ISBN 978 1 74270 822 5

Publishing Director: Paul McNally
Project Editor: Rihana Ries
Editor: Allison Hiew
Designer: Matthias Lanz/Loupe Studio
Photographer: Chris Middleton
Production Manager: Todd Rechner

Colour reproduction by Splitting Image Colour Studio
Printed and bound in China by 1010 Printing International Limited